A graduate of Harvard Divinity School, *Linnea Pearson* is currently involved in a campus ministry in Gainesville, Florida.

Ruth Bryant Purtilo is a trained physical therapist and a doctoral candidate in religious ethics at Harvard.

Separate Paths

1817

Published in San Francisco by

HARPER & ROW, PUBLISHERS

New York, Hagerstown, San Francisco, London

Separate Paths:

WHY PEOPLE END THEIR LIVES

By Linnea Pearson with Ruth Purtilo

Library of Congress Cataloging in Publication Data

Pearson, Linnea, 1939-
   SEPARATE PATHS.

   Includes bibliographical references.
   1. Suicide. I. Purtilo, Ruth, joint author.
II. Title.
HV6545.P4 1977   616.8'5844   77-23912
   ISBN 0-06-066481-9

This book is dedicated to PALCKF,
and to all those who wish to "see again."

Contents

Acknowledgements

OUR THANKS are due to the congregation of the Unitarian
Universalist Fellowship of Gainesville, Florida;
And to the following people who have offered us their
counsel and encouragement: Sandi Albertson, Joyce and
Allan Anderson, Anne and John Bennett, Susan Brenner,
Danice Bordett, Delores Brooks, Chris Cassel, Rosemary
Chinnici, Paul Clasper, Harvey Cox, Norman Faberow, J.
Fred, Brenda Goldberg, Joan and William Gurfield, Nancy
Hallinan, Mary Hunt, Marge Keip, Elisabeth
Kübler-Ross, Jean Lemark, Ruth Lewis, Bernie Loomer,
Carol Nawn, Diane Kennedy Pike, Elizabeth Sewell,
Huston Smith, William Stringfellow, Ernlé Young; and
especially, David Purtilo.
And to our mothers and fathers who have taught us so
much about life and death;
And to each other—for persevering through the dark spaces
and helping one another towards the light.

Old paint on canvas, as it ages, sometimes becomes transparent. When that happens it is possible, in some pictures, to see the original lines. . . . That is called pentimento because the painter "repented," changed his mind. Perhaps it would be as well to say that the old conception, replaced by a later choice, is a way of seeing and then seeing again.

From *Pentimento* by LILLIAN HELLMAN

PROLOGUE
A Voice for the Voiceless

THIS BOOK originated with an exchange of letters between
the authors about the suicide of a mutual friend. Their
correspondence continued and expanded into a general
discussion of the personal and theoretical issues involved in
suicide. That correspondence provided the basis for the
following exchange of letters which has been edited and
expanded to address issues not initially considered and to
interest a larger reading audience.

For purposes of this edited correspondence, and to
protect the confidences and interests of those personally
involved, the authors chose pseudonymns, one assuming the
character of student-questioner-seeker, the other the role of
professor-responder-counselor.

What will readily become evident, however, is the
interchange and exchange of these roles as the authors delve
deeper into the issue of suicide and all the questions they
find themselves asking each other.

In an effort to come closer to an understanding of the questions involved, Dr. Pearson has written a series of Reflections on the letters. These Reflections are intended to involve the reader more directly in the moral and personal issues raised but not resolved by the correspondence.

The issues are vital ones. Each year twice as many Americans kill themselves as kill each other. Experts estimate the number of suicides in America from 25,000 to 60,000 yearly and the number of attempted suicides to be at least 200,000.

Sociological tomes and psychological abstracts have been written on this phenomenon, but few books have been directly concerned with the emotions and sensitivities of the individuals involved and with the moral, ethical, religious, and theological interpretations of the suicide act.

The original impetus for this book came from the suicides in the winter of 1975 of Dr. Henry "Pit" Van Dusen, former president of Union Theological Seminary, and his wife, Elizabeth. Their suicide pact caused a great stir in the world of theology. In their suicide note, written by Elizabeth, they said, "We feel that this way we are taking will become more usual and acceptable as the years pass." The note ended with the quotation, "O Lamb of God that takest away the sins of the world / Have mercy upon us. / O Lamb of God that takest away the sins of the world / Grant us thy peace."

The use of these words from the Agnus Dei, so often a part of the traditional worship service, implies (1) that the Van Dusens believed that they were acting within the limits of religious community, and (2) that they had faith that their act would be forgiven, if need be—that they would be granted peace. Such beliefs as to the nature of suicide have seldom found a place within the boundaries of traditional faith and practice.

The purpose of this present study is to examine those

boundaries and definitions, and to attempt to break through these boundaries when the need to do so seems an ethical necessity. The process of establishing new boundaries can only be suggested here. This study is meant to be suggestive rather than definitive; provocative rather than positivistic; problematic, rather than dogmatic.

The authors do not offer any final solutions. They ask questions; they suggest approaches to reexamining the old taboos which have existed throughout written and unwritten history.

These taboos have kept suicide-as-topic locked in a closet. The authors are opening the closet. They believe that this process will offer new understanding to all who have contemplated suicide, to the survivors of suicide, and to all who care.

And who today, in this age of the Post-Human-Potential-Movement cannot care? For despite the latest therapies, guru movements, body-health cults, and consciousness-raising groups, many of us remain collectively or individually broken, not whole. Life is often not all it's cracked up to be. It is, in fact, quite "cracked" in many ways. Few of us believe that this is the best of all possible worlds, and it is easy to imagine some better ones in which pain, suffering, and injustice have no place.

Hamlet asked the question centuries ago: "To be or not to be?" The question has reverberated through the ages. Today one in every forty Americans decides every year at least tentatively "not to be" when he or she attempts suicide. It is estimated that the suicide rate of fifteen- to twenty-five-year-olds rose by 250 percent between 1960 and 1972. The director of the Los Angeles Suicide Prevention Center said recently at a meeting of the American Association of Suicidology, "I've never known a generation so interested in death as an experience, something you can pass through."[1]

Death, whether self-inflicted, accidental, natural, or unnatural, is part of the human experience. It is with the search for meaning in our common human experience that fundamental theology begins. This book is the start of a search to find the religious meaning of suicide—to place this long-taboo act within a context of moral, ethical, and theological thought, in which it is not simply dismissed as senseless, meaningless, or absurd.

Theologian Sally TeSelle has suggested that "our time may well be one of occasional theology, theology that is partial and particular, oriented to specific issues."[2] It is such a theology that this book is about.

We begin where we always begin, with raw human experience. In this case it is the news of the suicide of a young woman who seemed to have every motive for life—everything to live for—and yet killed herself. We proceed to an analysis, a synthesis, and a distillation of this raw experience in a search for meaning—the Reflections—which follow each exchange of letters.

For the purposes of this publication, the authors have assumed the pseudonyms and fictional identities of Christine Anderson and Rosa Harris. They have known each other for eight years, but in different roles; in different contexts; at times from different continents and cultures; and today from different parts of this continent: Cambridge, Massachusetts, and Berkeley, California.

Christine, the older woman, is in her mid-thirties. She teaches at Wellesley College, in the English Department. On an occasional and informal leave she lectures at other colleges; she is in demand as an academic who is also a person of warmth and understanding.

Originally, Christine's academic interests belonged to the traditional college curriculum: literature, humanities, poetry. But later she did post-doctoral studies in theology, and she is now planning for ordination as a Unitarian minister.

Rosa is twenty-nine and was at one time a student of Christine's. She is the daughter of a Minneapolis doctor, and comes from a traditionally conservative family. During her junior year at Wellesley she became visibly at odds with herself and life. Christine, her advisor, aware of her troubled state, invited her to dinner one night to talk about her problems. Thus their friendship began.

After graduation from Wellesley, Rosa began advanced work in a health-related field. She combined courses in anatomy, physiology, and psychology with a hospital job as a trainee therapist. She worked with young children at first; later with geriatric patients and terminally ill persons. This involved her in a lot of bedside care and family counseling, particularly with the bereaved. These experiences have led her back to doctoral work in clinical psychology at the University of California at Berkeley. She too is choosing a path.

Christine and Rosa are both practicing Christians; they are also questioning Christians with a passion for theology and semantics. The suicide of their mutual friend—a former student of Christine's and a dorm friend of Rosa's—triggers this particular exchange of letters. They want to make sense of Sarah's suicide. Does suicide make sense under certain circumstances and not under others? Is it against the law? Is it a crime? Is it a sin? Is suicide an act of martyrdom? Is it acceptable to God? Their friend's suicide leads them into a maze: paths leading this way and that way as they search for answers and find more and more questions.

As friends, Christine and Rosa are accustomed to separations and the changing roles that inevitably occur. Becuse of their many moves to different places, and the rising cost of phoning, they have become letter writers. They are increasingly aware, also of their great need to *record* experience. Thus their friendship has continued through the years on reams of typing paper. This correspondence focuses now on a certain person, Sarah, and then after her death, on the whole subject of suicide.

Sarah chose a certain path.

Her friends, Christine and Rosa, are the survivors. Their feelings about Sarah's suicide start them off on a journey, the outcome of which they cannot predict. As they discuss other famous suicides, such as Ernest Hemingway's and Marilyn Monroe's, they cannot escape their own feelings about life and death.

John Bennett, former president of Union Theological Seminary, said in an address to a divinity school audience in Berkeley, California: "The church must be the voice for all, especially for those who have no voice."

This was shortly after the Van Dusens' suicide. The day following Dr. Bennett's talk one of the authors of this book received the following letter in response to a recent speaking engagement:

> This letter is primarily to tell you what I thought of your talk and the reasons for my reactions. . . . My mother killed herself when I was ten. I am now twenty-three. The part of your talk that impressed me the most was when you talked about a person's right to kill himself and that it could be considered a rational decision on the part of the person to take a particular action. Until then, suicide had always been presented to me as something a person did in a moment of insanity or in a period of insanity, as something the person didn't really mean to do and wouldn't have done if he had been in his own right mind. And it is true that society looks down upon, avoids, and fears the family of a suicide, and the suicide himself. It is something to be ashamed of and hide. . . . I would be most interested to know if you have ideas about how society's attitudes toward suicide, and particularly towards the victim's family, can be changed. . . . I hope your book is

coming along well. . . . I think it will be a valuable piece of
writing.

Peace to you,
Bobbie Lindstrom

This book speaks for Bobbie Lindstrom and for her
family. It speaks for all those who have ended their own
lives, for the families and friends who have survived them,
and for all of those who have at one time or another
considered the deed themselves, know a friend or relative
who has, or may at some future time consider suicide.

The authors hope the reader will respond by asking more
questions and finding more answers. In other words by
continuing the dialogue which begins here.

CHAPTER 1

SARAH: *Death with Honor*

Sunday Morning
4 October
Berkeley, California

Dear Christine,

I have some bad news for you. I've tried to call you a dozen times in the last few hours, but I just remembered that you said in your last letter you'd be out of town giving a guest lecture.

I don't know how to tell you—maybe because this news is too painful for words—or maybe because it has never happened to someone so close before. Sarah took an overdose.

By the time we found her it was too late. She'd been dead for about seven or eight hours. I still can't believe it. Still don't truly believe it. Maybe I just *refuse* to believe it.

It happened Friday night. We had had supper in her room, a sandwich from the submarine shop where we three ate the last time you were here! I left for the library about eight. At ten she told Elizabeth she had an awful headache and was going to bed. Elizabeth was around all evening and didn't hear a sound from Sarah's room. Susan came in after midnight, saw a light on beneath the door, and knocked. Elizabeth told her that Sarah didn't want to be disturbed.

The next morning Elizabeth knocked at her door about nine. Still no answer. But Sarah used to sleep till about eleven on weekends. Around noon all three of us got worried. Maybe Sarah's severe headache had been a sign of food poisoning or something even worse. We knocked on her door *again.* Then we called her from Elizabeth's phone. We could hear the phone ringing. Finally we went to get Mrs. MacArthur to open the door. By then I was feeling really scared. The key turned; we peered in. There Sarah was on her bed—sprawled out in that long lavendar satiny robe she loved to wear. But her face was puffed and grey, her eyes closed, her auburn hair spread over the pillow. The lamp was on—the room unusually tidy—the drapes pulled.

Suddenly everyone started screaming, yelling at her and at each other. I tried desperately to regain my professional objectivity learned from my hospital days and I began mouth-to-mouth resuscitation. But there was no breath left. I don't think I'll ever forget the cold lips, slightly chapped and crackly, and the smell of my own breath returning mercilessly from the dead mouth. Mrs. MacArthur or somebody pulled me away. I found myself trembling from head to foot. Susan was sobbing hysterically, and Elizabeth just stared at me blindly. Mrs. MacArthur called the police, and her voice on the phone pulled us back to our senses.

There was a piece of paper in Sarah's typewriter. Elizabeth saw it first and took it out before the police came. When they asked if there'd been a note, we said no. Elizabeth kept silent. Later she gave it to me. It read:

To whoever finds me,
dear friends,
don't worry about me. i'm sorry to put you through all
this. just remember, it will soon be over. i've
decided it's the best way for me now. i don't like any
of the alternatives. this has the advantage of honor—
death with honor—"a consummation devoutly to be wished"—
and is better than life with dishonor. i don't blame
geoff; he did what he had to do. i don't blame my folks;
they are what they are. i ask that none of you blame me;
i am what i am; i do what i must do.
wish me well, as i do you.
we all have our separate paths—we shall meet again.
sarah.

They took her away. When everyone else had left
Sarah's room, Elizabeth and I stayed and talked about the
note. We were propped up on pillows in Sarah's room as if
—as if maybe she'd come running through the door. The
note baffled us—so unlike the Sarah we'd thought we'd
known—the Sarah who would scoff at words like *honor,* and
often alienated people with her willfulness and her adamant
positions on intellectual issues! How *little* we knew the real
Sarah! I remember doing strange things like going over to
her plants and touching the soil; it was damp—she had
watered them that night! Then I picked at a tuft in her
patchwork quilt and shuffled through a pile of papers on her
bedside table. I remember holding her alarm clock to my ear.
That persistent ticking! I thought how strange it was that all
of these objects in Sarah's life kept going on despite her
death, and how strange that she should die in a dormitory
like that with all of us around her.

You can imagine the atmosphere here today. In one way
her death has brought us closer together. Imagine Karl and
me embracing in the corridor! My memory of his brother's
recent suicide was so much more important than our mutual

and usual hostility. We're sobered too. We all feel somehow it's our own fault. Elizabeth keeps insisting that she could have prevented it—since she was the last person to see Sarah alive. (When she first said that, I was so dumbfounded I just gaped at her, and before I could say a word she left the room, slamming the door behind her.) Mrs. MacArthur feels that everyone is pointing at *her* since she's the official dorm supervisor.

But Christine, one reason I'm so anxious to reach you is that I feel it's *my* fault. Maybe if I tell you why I feel so terrible you can help me sort it out.

Well, everyone knew that Sarah's relationship with her parents was strained. She simply couldn't accept their values. And she made it clear to them that she was no longer the nice Methodist girl they wanted her to be. So some people think her death had something to do with them. A few knew that Geoff had split, and they are sure she did it because of him. But I knew something about Sarah no one else knew. And I keep thinking that if . . .

About a week ago she knocked on my door and asked if I was in the mood for a little confidential chat. I said sure and invited her in. She had barely closed the door when she said in that offhand way of hers, "I'm pregnant. Three months." Geoff (you met Geoff last spring, didn't you?) had decided he wasn't ready for marriage. So when he took off for Atlanta, Sarah had told everybody they needed some time apart, and his offer of a government fellowship would provide that opportunity.

I asked her what she planned to do. She was acting so matter-of-factly about the whole thing that I thought this might get her in touch with what seemed to be a serious situation. She said she'd decided to get an abortion; she knew that would be easiest. She had already gone to one of the women's centers here (a good one, too), and said she'd discussed it with a counselor. She shrugged her shoulders and said in that tough-talking way of hers, "This is quick." Also, she didn't want the child without Geoff and didn't want to raise it alone. Then I asked her if she'd discussed this with her parents. She stared at the leaves outside my window. (They're beginning to turn golden already!) Finally she shook her head. We just sat there silently. I felt paralyzed. I felt her pain, saw it, felt waves of it flow through me. Suddenly the telephone rang—a long distance call from a friend of mine who had just been appointed to the University of Kansas Medical School faculty. She was elated, of course, and by the time I was able to tell her I was busy and would call back, Sarah had signaled goodbye.

Last Wednesday about seven she came to my room again. I told her I was late for my ethics lecture but maybe we could talk later. She shrugged and said it didn't matter, then smiled that devil-may-care smile of hers and sauntered out of the room. I was sort of relieved.

But that was the last time I saw her alive. Oh Christine, I feel such guilt. Of course she wanted to talk or she wouldn't have come. On the other hand, I could say that it was her responsibility to show up and talk. And now *I* feel such pain. And awe too.

I dreamed last night that she was shouting to me from the dorm kitchen. In my dream I put on my robe and went out into the corridor. The lights in the corridor were out—it was a moist, oppressive darkness—and I was frightened. I knew that she was calling from behind the door in the little side storage room. When I peered into the room still guided by her voice—very loud now and frightening—I was seized with horror. The room was empty. I woke up in a cold sweat, unable to go back to sleep and afraid, too.

I still feel strange. As you know, I'm living back in the same room this fall and no longer feeling awkward at being an older student in the graduate dorm. You see, part of my decision to come back to the dorm was based on knowing that Sarah would be back. (Since I'm twenty-nine and Sarah was twenty-four, it seemed we could support one another as "older women.") And last night when her phone rang I expected for a moment that she would answer it. It was like getting the news for the first time all over again when the ringing went on and on.

Well, you can see I can't make any sense of this event—nothing but the horrible waste of this bright, beautiful young woman's life. I'm turning to you for comfort and also hoping you can clear up some of the questions that haunt me. For instance, knowing how deeply she trusted you, I can't help wondering if she might have written to you about Geoff and her pregnancy. Did she share this?

There's no conventional ending to such a letter.

Adieu for now.
Rosa

P.S. Do you know—a horrible realization—I see now that I have just taken Sarah really seriously for the first time! She was always so self-dramatizing. I always thought of her as a real actress on the stage of life—one who had her act perfected better than most. But I've just understood, Christine—*I never took her seriously till now.*

20 October, Sunday
Cambridge, Massachusetts

Dear Rosa,

Just back in town late last night. Speaking engagements, yes, in Florida and Georgia. Your letter was here, but I didn't open it till this morning.

Sarah's suicide. A part of me simply can't respond to the fact. I've reread your letter three times, picked up the phone twice to talk to you, but . . . it would have been just dawn in Berkeley and, besides, I *didn't know what to say.* A part of me simply wails in anguish. Then I keep hearing Jesus' words on the Cross—"My God, my God, why hast thou forsaken me?"

Yes, I knew about Sarah's pregnancy. And about Geoff's leaving. Sarah wrote me about it all last month—just before I was leaving for this lecture tour. I was so busy preparing that I just put it aside. It's on my desk right now. Waiting for an answer.

So now I join the chorus of those of you who feel guilty. "What if . . ." "If only I had answered . . ." Well, I'm also shocked. I didn't think she had it in her. Sarah always seemed able to cope—either with an offhand, cynical, humorous remark, or with a blasé manner that implied firsthand knowledge of the absurd.

Yet none of that shows up in her note. Who would have suspected Sarah to be worrying about "death with honor" and "life with dishonor"? Not me, certainly. And I was her *teacher* for over a year, her confidante and general unofficial counselor.

She had confided to me the experience of her grandfather's suicide death last Christmas. He'd been living all alone in Miami. Too proud and perhaps too wise to go to a nursing home. He was in pretty good health, so there was no real need for nursing care.

When Sarah visited him last Thanksgiving, they had a truly amazing conversation. Sarah said he swore her to confidence (she was always his favorite grandchild and he actually felt closer to her than to any of his own children) and to non-intervention. Then he told her that he planned to kill himself within the next few weeks—after he'd said all his goodbyes.

Sarah said he had it all figured out quite rationally. There was nothing he really enjoyed doing any more. He had passed on the family business to his son (Sarah's father), and the business was doing well. He missed his wife a great deal; she had died the previous year. All that he felt he could provide now for anyone was an occasional place to visit. And that was well and good, but chances were great that a stroke or some fatal disease would overtake him eventually, and then he might not have the chance to make the decision he was now able to make and to act upon.

He was telling Sarah so that she wouldn't be hurt by the shock of it; so that she could help give comfort to the others after the fact (assure them that it was a rational decision, etc.), and to in effect ask her blessing. Sarah reported the meeting between them to me as "one of the most meaningful events of my life." She said she had felt, "for the first time like an adult, face to face with the most adult realization any of us has to confront—death, and its inevitability for us all."

She said that after that his actual self-inflicted death was not a burden to her. She said she had felt blessed by his caring for her enough to take her into his trust in that way; it had been *that* that had been important to her.

But now I know I didn't listen closely enough to everything Sarah said about her grandfather's death. I wasn't sensitive to how profound an effect it must have had on her. Now I really feel her suicide must have been directly related to his choice and to her identification with him—her love for him.

I'm afraid now, in retrospect, there were many times when I didn't listen well enough to Sarah—didn't push her to speak of difficult but important matters. I'm afraid I've always considered Sarah as "the rich girl" who had had all the advantages I wished I had had. All the right schools; her Shaker Heights family status. She and her parents traveled around the world together three times. She'd studied at the Sorbonne as an exchange student; for her last birthday her parents had given her a new Granada. She had all the advantages—everything money could buy—and seemed to take it all for granted. I think I assumed that our teacher-student, counselor-counselee relationship was not to be taken *too* seriously, because if anything *really* serious came up, she'd go to the best psychiatrist in California.

Well now, dear Rosa, you are looking to me for comfort, and I am doing, instead, my own mea culpa, so this must stop.

Also, dear friend, you must know it's NOT your fault. It was Sarah's decision; she must bear the responsibility. In the final analysis, we are all responsible for ourselves. If she'd really wanted to talk to you more, it was her responsibility to push you to it. We choose our counselors with great purpose. Something in Sarah made her choose you, perhaps just because she knew you would *not* be available. She could have gone to Mrs. MacArthur—Mrs. MacArthur is *always* there, as you know! She could have gone to Elizabeth. She could have called *me* on the phone! She could have gone to some faculty member or to someone in her church. Or any of the free counseling facilities available there! No, it was *not* your fault! Sarah died because she did not want to live any longer. Whether you had or had not answered the phone or gone to your ethics class or whatever would not have made any difference.

But the baby—that's another matter. I begin to think about the thousands of women who die trying to abort themselves. In Sarah's letter she asked me what I thought about abortion. Now, as you know, I've worked long and hard to get the law changed so that having an abortion would be no longer illegal. My position was that it should be a matter between the woman herself, her doctor, and her God—and her man if he were still around. And for two reasons. First as a principle of law, the separation of church and state. Second, because of the thousands of women who die each year as the result of being butchered by illegal abortionists.

But to say "I believe in abortion" is a different matter. I've always felt that no one should tell another woman that she *must* bear a child unless that other person is willing to take responsibility for the life of that child after it is born. So could I, would I, have had the courage to tell Sarah, "I understand your doubts about having the child. So let me suggest this—that you come and stay with me for the next few months, away from where you are known, where you can continue your studies, where I can give you emotional and physical support, and then, after the baby is born, I will assume responsibility for him or her"?

That, dear Rosa, I believe would have been the only truly moral response to her letter. And that is why I put off answering. I didn't want the responsibility. So I feel I've also let Sarah down. Yet I know this isn't rational—any more than your own guilt.

One word of possible comfort. I still don't see Sarah's suicide in the terms you do—as "the horrible waste of this bright, beautiful young woman's life." I do see some nobility in the death itself which has a certain power to it I never realized in Sarah. Does this sound cold and hard?

And your postscript. "I never took her seriously till now!" I wonder if somehow she has not achieved in her death what she would never have achieved in her life. Heidegger speaks of the difference between seeing life as just a series-of-functions-leading-to-death, and seeing life as a series of symbolic acts leading to a symbolic death and what Christians call the resurrection.

I wonder if we can't see Sarah's death as a sort of symbolic act which points beyond itself to some greater hope. "We all have our separate paths." And then, "We shall meet again." Is it not significant that those were her last written words? Can't we see Sarah's death as a statement of hope—as well as an act of honor? How do we know that this was *not* the right time for Sarah? Here I am responding to your questions by just raising more of my own. But how hard it is to make sense of our lives. I'm thinking about my high school days when one of those glory-bearing football players, everyone's idol, drove his motorcycle into a brick wall after his girl, whom he was engaged to marry, went out with another member of the team. *Nobody could believe it.* Here was this fellow who could have any girl he wanted killing himself over Cherie, a little blonde cheerleader. He also left a note: "Cherie, I loved you. You made a fool of me. Jim."

That note, Rosa, taught me even as a teenager that love is not something to be played around with. I guess that's why I could never really get into the sexual revolution and the whole playboy ethic. I knew at an early age that people could die—could literally kill themselves—for love—in *real life!* And that's made me take love seriously, and stand with those who consider love and loving covenantal relationships to be in some way sacred.

You closed your letter with *adieu.* Did you know that that comes from the old French way of saying goodbye, translated, "Till we meet at the feet *of God,*" or *"à dieu"*?

Do give my love, my condolences, to everyone there.

Also, do you have Sarah's parents' address? And where is Geoff? Does *he* know? Write soon.

Affectionately,
Christine

REFLECTIONS

IN EACH of these commentaries our three principal concerns will be: (1) the effect the suicide event had on Rosa and Christine, (2) the meaning the suicide seemed to have had to the suicidee,[1] (3) the significance of the act in terms of society and the community to which the individuals belonged.

Rosa's first letter, written three days after Sarah's suicide, is filled with exclamations of wonder and amazement—"I still can't believe it"; descriptions of the terror of death, especially the unexpected, untimely death—"Everyone started screaming and yelling"; expressions of great guilt—"I can't help thinking it's *my* fault." Eventually she admits, "I can't make any sense of this event." She tries to put the pieces together; she lists the prosaic events of Friday evening, the suicide discovery, Sarah's previous confessions, the details of the room. Rosa's reaction here is similar to that experienced by many of us at the news of another's death. We find comfort by anchoring in physical, concrete details when in the presence of the ultimate abstract mystery. If we can find a How or a Why to someone's death, then we can file it neatly away under L for leukemia or A for auto accident. But there is no such comfort in S for Suicide. The "Why?" remains unanswered.

Rosa's letter is also concerned with this mystery and strangeness. "Strange that she should die in a dormitory like that, with all of us around her." But, of course, it is not strange. All of us die, will die, surrounded by others who remain in life.

Part of the strangeness of the suicide is that it often takes place outside of the hospital. Our sensibilities are affronted when we are forced to face death on our home ground; we feel that it is an invasion of territory. How dare the dead encroach upon the land of the living! If death can strike in the dormitory room next to mine, it can strike anywhere—perhaps even in my room! This is too close, too close for comfort.

Another element of the strangeness of the suicide is that it gives us no time for preparation. We can rarely say of a suicide, as we can of the death at the end of a long illness, "We expected it." Death by suicide catches us off guard; we have no time to build psychic defenses against it; there is no gradual fading away, no convenient bacteria to blame it on; it fails to fit any of our preordained logic. It is "unnatural."

The world of suicide is a world "out of joint" where none of our regular paradigms work. It is a world with no structures, no context for our experience. Much has been written on the sociological significance and psychological interpretations of suicide, but nobody has succeeded in answering the real question—"Why?—or its corrollary—"Why not?" The unspoken assumption of sociologists, psychologists, and theologians alike has always been that suicide is "wrong."

This assumption is partly shared but also partly questioned by Rosa's teacher-friend Christine. Christine's letter reveals guilt feelings that she too could have done something to prevent Sarah's suicide; and then she wonders about the possible rightness of Sarah's decision, realizing that she sees "some nobility in the deed itself . . . a power . . . never realized in Sarah." Death brings no answers to her, but it does offer new awareness of previously hidden realities.

This new awareness that sudden death can bring is
expressed by Edwin Arlington Robinson in his poem,
"Richard Cory":

Whenever Richard Cory went down town
    We people on the pavement looked at him:
He was a gentleman from sole to crown,
    Clean favored, and imperially slim.

And he was always quietly arrayed,
    And he was always human when he talked;
But still he fluttered pulses when he said,
    "Good-morning," and he glittered when he walked.

And he was rich—yes, richer than a king,
    And admirably schooled in every grace:
In fine, we thought that he was everything
    To make us wish that we were in his place.

So on we worked, and waited for the light,
    And went without the meat, and cursed the bread;
And Richard Cory, one calm summer night,
    Went home and put a bullet through his head.[2]

How appearance and reality so seldom correlate! Richard
Cory's suicide reveals the way in which such a self-chosen
death can offer the survivors not answers, but new
awareness which is in itself a kind of truth.

The townspeople in "Richard Cory" judged the man only
by his wealthy appearance. Christine assumed somewhat
resentfully that Sarah had "everything money could buy."
But what Sarah's death-by-suicide told Christine was
something else, a message she didn't want to hear. Most of
us don't want to hear it.

We prefer to hold to our illusions of human happiness
being not only possible and attainable, but also the norm,
the happy ending just around the corner. Thus we assume

that life is always preferable to death. We have lost the faith of the early Christian martyrs who believed that the true glory was in the life-to-come. We believe that any soul-sickness such as might lead to suicide should be curable, if only we had the right medicine for it—the proper miracle drugs or tranquilizers.

We want to believe that the status quo is OK. Or, at least, remediable. To a large extent, many of us have been fed and have incorporated the belief that "everyday in everyway, things are getting better and better." The suicide denies the hope that the status quo will improve or change at all. We don't want to believe that the world is irremediably out of joint. We want to believe that if we just try hard enough we can set it right.

So a suicide comes as a sort of Final Judgment. And the fear we feel is the loss of our ability to touch or be touched by the suicide. We also fear that the day may come when no one around may be response-able to us.

For most of us the ultimate horror is total isolation. Thus the worst punishment in most prisons, the most brutal torture tactic in most war camps, has always been "the hole," solitary confinement. Similarly, the horror we feel toward the suicidee is twofold: first, that he or she did not feel our accepting responsiveness, and second, that he or she no longer saw anything truly worth responding to in us.

Christine's ambiguous feelings towards Sarah were based in part on her own ambivalent feelings towards the supposed invulnerability that wealth brings. Similarly, Rosa's failure to respond to the conflict within Sarah may be seen as indicative of her failure to respond to the conflict within herself between the same issues Sarah was faced with —i.e. those of following or rejecting the traditional mores For Rosa like Sarah is a young woman caught in the perils of a time "out of joint."

Both are modern, liberated women. How do the old

values of love, marriage, childbearing, "woman's place," correlate with the new values? Or do they? We can see both Christine and Rosa beginning to reexamine the old injunction to love our neighbors as ourselves. And they begin by responding to Sarah's death with the realization of what has died in them—the realization that the part of themselves which Sarah represented to them was unloved or unaccepted in themselves, and thus they rejected it in Sarah. Sarah's real death then is forcing them to examine the rejected parts of themselves, their own conflicts between accepting and rejecting the values of society. Sarah was unmarried and pregnant at twenty-five. According to the standards of the new society she could have had an abortion and gone on her way. According to the standards of the old society of her family she was a "fallen woman." She was caught between two worlds. Caught in the middle, she didn't like any of the alternatives.

One of the questions we must ask about Sarah's death is in what way it was a statement about her life, a statement that perhaps she could not have made in any other way. Our immediate, conditioned response to the suicide of a young person is that it is wasteful. Perhaps that is a premise we need to reconsider.

We might ask, "What if Sarah had decided to live out the rest of her life?" But this implies that she had a rest of her life. How do we know? To admit the possible rightness of her act, to give her the benefit of the doubt, we must grant the possibility that this was her right time to die.

We could, of course, hypothesize a future for Sarah. She could have had an abortion and gone on to get her Ph.D. and become a college professor. She could have had the baby and become reconciled with Geoff and become a happy or unhappy housewife. But how can we judge that any one of these scenarios would have been the right one?

Who has the right to make that decision? To pronounce

that judgment? To whom did Sarah's life belong? To the state? To her parents? To her lover? To her unborn child? To her friends? To God? To herself?

These are some of the basic questions we will be considering throughout this book. The traditional Christian funeral service has in it the words, "The Lord giveth and the Lord taketh away; blessed be the name of the Lord." But Jesus insisted that he himself was in charge of his own life: "For this reason the Father loves me, because I lay down my life. . . . No one takes it from me, but I lay it down of my own accord" (John 10:17–18).[3]

Did Sarah have that same right? Do any or all of us have that same right and privilege? Or were there extenuating circumstances in the case of Jesus that do not apply to us?

Sarah obviously felt she had the right. And also the need: "I do what I must do." Are we to judge that she was wrong? If so, on what bases?

Her note has in it five basic elements: the giving of forgiveness (to Geoff and her parents); the asking of forgiveness ("I ask that none of you blame me"); the desire for a "death with honor"; the insistence that this is a thought-full decision ("I don't like any of the alternatives"); and the faith in a future meeting ("We shall meet again"), which clearly seems to point to a hope in the communal resurrection believed in by the early Church, a resurrection hope or belief in an afterlife common also to many other religions.

"We all have our separate paths—we shall meet again." Thus she ends her note, bringing to mind Jesus' statement to his disciples just before Judas' betrayal of him. Judas has left the dinner room and Jesus says to those who remain, "Yet a little while am I with you. . . . Where I am going you cannot follow me now; but you shall follow me afterward" (John 14:2). None of his friends understand what he means.

Thomas asks, "Lord, we do not know where you are

going; how can we know the way?" Jesus answers, "I am the way." Then it is Philip who is uncomprehending. And Jesus says to him, with great sadness, "Have I been with you so long, and yet you do not know me?" (John 14:9).

When Sarah wrote, "We shall meet again," she may well have had this scenario in mind. For here Jesus is facing the fact of betrayal, denial, misunderstanding, and rejection by those closest to him, by those whom he had chosen to be his friends, those whom he might have thought would have known better. Surely Sarah might have been experiencing the same disappointment in those she had appointed in her life to be her closest friends and confidantes. And perhaps she experienced the same awareness, or at least hope, that when they would "meet again," the knowledge would be complete.

Certainly with Sarah there was a sense in which those closest to her understood her most fully only after her death. Rosa says, "I've just understood . . . I never took her seriously till now!" Christine says, "I do see some nobility in the deed which . . . I never realized in Sarah." How often only death lets us know more of another person's total reality in a way that allows us to take him or her seriously! Love and death are also related in this way, for we cannot love someone without taking their reality "deadly seriously!"

Love and death—the two great teachers. In the Bible the verb "to know," used in the sense of knowing another person, means "to have sexual relations with." The one or more persons with whom we are most intimate in our lifetimes are the ones we "know" sexually. Although psychological and physical pretense may still remain, it becomes much less likely with physical nakedness and the resultant vulnerability and openness to another that is part of true sexual intimacy.

Thus the great mystics in almost all religious traditions often use explicit sexual imagery when analogizing their relationship to, their knowledge of, God. And so the story of the Garden of Eden tells us that it was at the moment that Adam and Eve ate of the Tree of Knowledge that they became aware of their sexuality and also of their mortality. We are told that they never did eat of the Tree of Life in order that "they might live forever." Similarly, we are told by the scientists that it is only among the higher, i.e., more complex, forms of life that we find both male and female sexuality and, also, death (asexual atoms and amoebas, for all we know, may go on forever).

So, for humankind, love and death are intricately related. Love, the conscious intimate relationship with another person which results in some form of creativity, and death, which is given meaning and therefore made bearable by love, remain the two great powers, the two great mysteries, and the two great teachers. Thus, traditionally, love and death have been the bases of most church sacraments. Lovers of mortals and martyrs for God have both lived and died for love, and the reality of love has been taken with "deadly seriousness."

But in our society both love and death have been seriously cheapened. Many wedding ceremonies no longer include the vow to love "till death do us part—and even then do I pledge you my love." The current assumption, as the host of a California radio show says, is that "No relationship lasts forever." The modern creed has become that displayed on many popular posters: "You go your way and I go mine, and if by chance we meet, it's beautiful, and if not it can't be helped." This indifference to the sanctity of human love, human relationships, and human interrelatedness is not new in our culture. But it has reached epidemic proportions (see Philip Slater's *The Pursuit of Loneliness*). And it is clearly antireligious (*religion* from the root word *religare*—meaning "to tie together as with sheaves of wheat") in its orientation.

It is this sort of ideological disclaimer of the interrelatedness of us all that we may imagine the Pharisee saying to the man who had fallen among robbers on the road from Jerusalem to Jericho. Or the dwellers in the New York high-rise saying to the woman being stabbed in their parking lot. Or, in this instance, Geoff saying to Sarah. How do we live and die with honor in such a world?

Sarah chose the way that seemed most honorable to her. Who is to say that she was wrong?

CHAPTER 2

CHARLOTTE PERKINS GILMAN:

An End to Social Usefulness

1 November
Berkeley

Dear Christine,

Your letter was such a comfort! That you knew about Sarah's pregnancy and Geoff, and that I wasn't the only one.

There are so many lessons to learn from this experience! For one, not to take another person's problems quite so casually. For another, to listen more closely, be a little more sensitive. You really hit home to me when you said that the "really moral thing" would have been to have asked Sarah to come to Boston, so that you could provide literal protection and support for her at that time. That seems to me to be the "really moral thing" too. But how many of us would be willing to do it—to accept such a burden?

Oh, so many unanswered questions! You suggested that her suicide had an element of nobility in it. And Heidegger says a death might be a symbolic act pointing to some greater hope. But a part of me suspects that Sarah's death was *ignoble,* and that haunts me. Yes, I *did* take her seriously for the first time after she killed herself, but how I wish I'd taken her seriously before!

Yes, I agree now that Sarah has to take the responsibility for her act herself. But what about *our* responsibility? "Any man's [or woman's] death diminishes me, because I am involved in Mankinde." If Donne is right, how can Sarah die without having it significantly affect my life/death too?

Enough! I want to bring you *really* up to date. Ironic life! Sarah has become a local folk heroine. She's talked about everywhere; one hears her name in coffeeshop rap sessions, outside classrooms. A poem was dedicated to her in the *Uni-News.* And a fund has been set up *in her name* by an endowment from her parents to develop a suicide prevention center on campus.

You guessed it. I've been asked to serve on the planning committee. Also, because I knew Sarah better than some (and maybe because of my previous hospital work), quite a few students have come to me wanting to talk. They *say* they want to make some sense out of what happened to Sarah. But I think they want to explore their own fears of and feelings about suicide. A tough job. When some of them go on about Sarah's virtues, I keep remembering the very different things they said about her when she was alive. Sometimes I'm angry at Sarah for putting me in this position—she gets all the attention and I'm supposed to defend her! I'm literally *obsessed* with this whole suicide question. I'm having trouble keeping my mind on my regular work (my clinical psych class is a disaster! As for ethics—!). For instance, I daydream about how I would kill myself if I decided to commit suicide. (Curious, that word *commit*—as if it were a crime!) I have fantasies about how people would react if they found me strung up from the commonroom chandelier some morning, or dead on my bed the way Sarah was dead on hers. Who would find me and how, and how would the news spread? How would my suicide affect my friends. And—Paul! Would they be upset? For how long? One night I became really frightened! I felt all of the energy and interest had already been spent on Sarah, and that if I killed myself, *I* would be just a *statistic.* (Christine, don't worry! These feelings are just exhaustion.)

Well, you asked about Geoff. He went off to Georgia as planned for his year of work and study, and is still there for all I know. I've heard no more.

Your news about Sarah's grandfather came as a real shock. She admired him. She talked of him often, but not one word to me about his suicide.

Now one of my digressions—except it's not really a digression. My Woman's Study course has had me researching the early American suffragettes. And I came across a suicide. (Not the famous one when the woman threw herself in front of a racehorse, but a very different sort.) Charlotte Perkins Gilman. Have you heard of her? She was a leader in the woman's suffrage movement in the early 1900s, and took her own life when she was told she had cancer. There is very little written about her. The article on her death in the *New York Times* of 20 August 1935, was buried on page 44 three days after her death—on the same day that the front-page headline held the news of the death of Will Rogers and Wiley Post in an air crash in Alaska. The headline showed society's need for easy explanations: "Charlotte Gilman Dies to Avoid Pain," it read. Untrue, untrue! But, the subhead reported more honestly her assertion that suicide was "the simplest of human rights." Untrue?

Her suicide note fascinates me. It's a marvel of the cool-headed rationalism that apparently Sarah's grandfather also had. Here's Gilman's note, found beside her body after she had killed herself by taking chloroform. (She was seventy-five.)

> No grief, pain, misfortune or "broken heart" is excuse for cutting off one's life while any power of service remains.
> But when all usefulness is over, when one is assured of an unavoidable and imminent death, it is the simplest of human rights to choose a quick and easy death in place of a slow and horrible one.
> Public opinion is changing on the subject. The time is approaching when we shall consider it abhorrent to our civilization to allow a human being to die in prolonged agony which we should mercifully end in any other creature.
> Believing this choice to be of social service in promoting wiser views on this question, I have preferred Chloroform to cancer.[1]

In a follow-up article the next day, Mrs. Carrie Chapman Catt, then seventy-six, one of Mrs. Gilman's sister suffragettes who had previously named her as one of the twelve greatest American women, said of Mrs. Gilman's suicide:

> I think it is cowardly in general when people take their own lives and dodge all their responsibilities. . . . But she was afflicted with an incurable malady, and the doctors said she might live two months. What she did was not to take her life, but merely to cut it short by a very brief period. It was not cowardice as suicide is when people are afraid. She would have gone on as long as she could have been of any service to the world. She was a great woman. . . . A woman of her vigor would do exactly that thing to avoid trouble to her daughter, with whom she lived.

The library microfilmed copies of the Gilman suicide note and Mrs. Catt's newspaper statement lie on my desk among the clutter of papers, unanswered letters, and *endless* memoranda on the Suicide Prevention Center. And it's those old clippings that are making me pause and think.

Christine, maybe Sarah's and Charlotte Gilman's suicide notes point to a mutual need—to be respected and accepted. Sarah speaks of it as "honor" and Charlotte Gilman as "usefulness." Gilman obviously feels that if a person can't serve others, then life isn't worthwhile. I've often heard this in hospitals when people become limited by sickness or disability. Christine, I believe modern society makes people believe that a person's worth is measured by his/her industry, autonomy, or/and productivity! Idleness is wickedness. If you're not useful anymore, you aren't worth keeping. So some people decide to kill themselves when they are no longer useful! But imagine the conflict if they are within the Judeo-Christian tradition! The Jewish law forbids it outright. And the Christian position is no less adamant—one of the reasons being that suicide is an act contrary to sustaining life-in-community. I guess Charlotte Gilman thought that to sustain life-in-community she had to be of service to others. She equated the *dignity* of life with the *usefulness* of life. I know a lot of people do that. You and me too! But who can define what usefulness is? Can the person be the sole judge of his or her own usefulness? If not, who can? The person's family or friends? A doctor? A government agency? Besides, if *usefulness* makes life worthwhile, gives it dignity, what happens to the person who becomes useless but doesn't want to kill him or herself? Should he/she be treated as less-than-human? Be killed? Be *forced* to commit suicide?

The most haunting example for me concerns a young woman whom I treated after she became paralyzed in a car accident. All she could move was her head. She was a young widow with three small children (her husband was killed in Vietnam), so you would think she might have felt the need to go on living for the sake of the little ones. However, she felt that as a quadriplegic she was nothing but a burden.

She asked all of us who treated her to please help her kill herself. We all refused. Well, it's not easy to kill yourself when all you can move is your head, but one night she managed to turn her head around far enough to reach her hand. She killed herself by chewing off her numb fingers and strangling on them. The whole hospital staff was stunned. I remember having nightmares of finding her totally dismembered in some frantic attempt to destroy herself. We asked ourselves again and again what we might have done differently.

Of course I remember scores of people who were just as much (or more) of a "burden" but who had a tremendous love of life. So why do some kill themselves? Maybe because there was no real balance in their lives between giving and taking. A community should be a place for receiving others' care as well as giving. It should be a place for love to be shown to the weak and suffering. If anyone who can no longer *give* kills him or herself, isn't that depriving others of learning to minister, to give? Didn't Jesus ask for help—food, a drink of water, emotional support, when he was weak?

Back to Sarah's grandfather. Do you think she felt he really wanted her to talk him out of his death? As I'm learning, most suicides give out clues to those they care about before killing themselves. And I'm coming to believe that often when someone says that he/she is not worthwhile (i.e., ugly, useless, old), we tend to neglect or ignore it. Christine, I really think suicide in general is a statement about a society where something has gone very wrong. What do you think?

I know what *I* think. And believe. I believe our lives are *a gift from God.* I am so often eye to eye with the mystery of birth and death, sickness and health, that I am convinced that the dignity of life has more value than any sum of qualities we ascribe to it. It is more than usefulness, state of health, age, sex, financial status, etc. I have watched patients with painful terminal illnesses "come to life" and experience, or so they say, the best part of their lives, while the so-called "healthy" are sometimes work-driven or barbituate-calm ghosts in fashionable funeral clothes. To me, life is *simply and solely* worthwhile on the basis that it is human life.

Life!

And since today is All Saint's Day I will end by saying, "All the Saints Greet You!" especially those unrecognized by any of the authorities! And bless you for your letter. Write soon.

Adieu,
Rosa

Dear Rosa,

Thank you for your All Saints Day letter. And apologies for my late reply. Actually I started several letters to you but they ended up in wadded balls in my wastepaper basket.

Dear friend, what's going on with you? What's all this talk about imagining your own suicide? I can understand your anger at Sarah for disappearing and leaving all the unfinished business of her life to you to clear up. And I can understand your resentment at those who come to you and impose on your time and strength for help in coping with their own guilts about Sarah's death. And I can understand your feeling that you must not reject them as you feel you rejected Sarah. But something's going on you're not telling me. What's happening out there? How are classes? Have you thought of consulting a therapist? (I could suggest one or two.) How much of the guilt over Sarah's death are you still taking upon yourself?

Back here in Massachusetts it is almost Thanksgiving again. And I can't help remembering the events of last Thanksgiving—Sarah with her grandfather discussing his suicide. If that hadn't happened, would she still be alive? We do know that suicidal parents often produce suicidal children. The most famous example in our time is Ernest Hemingway. To what extent did his father's suicide trigger his own?

One of my friends at Harvard Medical School, when I told him about Sarah, brought me a copy of the following from the *Medical Record* of 26 October 1901:

A man named Edgar Jay Briggs, who hanged himself on his farm, near Danbury, Connecticut, a few days ago, was almost the last surviving member of a family which has practically been wiped out of existence by suicide. The history of self-destruction in this family extends over a period of more than fifty years, and in that time, so it is stated, at least twenty-one of the descendants and collaterals of the original Briggs suicide have taken their own lives. Among these were the great-grandfather, grandfather, father, brother, and two sisters of the one just dead. Many of the suicides were effected in an unusual way. One man drowned himself by holding his face in a shallow brook, another attached a weight to a collar about his neck and then waded into a pond. Others shot or hanged themselves in a way evidencing fixed determination to end their lives. All of the suicides were not blood relations, some being women who had married into the family.[2]

If Sarah's grandfather had not killed himself, what about Sarah?

This is the start of the holiday season. According to many studies more people commit suicide during the holidays than at any other time. Why? Probably because people's expectations are so great, and the reality so disappointing. The world is out of joint with their idealized vision of it.

This will be my first Thanksgiving without Michael. I'm trying not to relive the news of that automobile accident just before Christmas last year. I don't quite know how to handle this holiday. One doesn't make Thanksgiving dinner for one's self! And I have tried not to present myself as "widow" to the college community here. Still, I grieve that Michael and I had such a short time together. And with Sarah's suicide so much on my mind, I'm wondering more and more how accidental his death was.

The effect of Michael's death on the community here was one of shocked and discreet silence. Very different from the effect of Sarah's death at Berkeley. Now she's a folk heroine! Well, Berkeley always has been different from Cambridge. Still, I am suspicious of this glorification of the macabre.

What about this new suicide prevention center being financed by Sarah's folks? How much of this is blood money to assuage their guilt? (Even so, the result could be good, of course.) But what does the suicide prevention center *do?* Does it serve to perpetuate the taboos against suicide? Does it encourage people to take responsibility for the lives you "save"?

I'm reminded of one of Kurt Vonnegut's books in which he writes of "suicide parlors" established to help people who have decided to end their lives. At these parlors, they are treated well, have all their last wishes met, and then are aided in ending their lives in the most gentle ways possible. Daniel Stern played with much the same idea in his recent novel, *The Suicide Academy.* Then not too long ago, some young enterprising man down south tried to start such a place. It was, of course, promptly shut down by the police.

I was fascinated by your tale of the suffragette. And I agree with you about the parallels you noticed between Charlotte Gilman's death and that of Sarah's grandfather. I am sure both felt an end to social usefulness. But on the other hand, because of Mrs. Gilman's illness and her greater social prominence, I believe she saw her death much more as a "witness" than did Sarah's grandfather. According to her note, she killed herself "believing this choice to be of social service." (An act of community good.) I was also intrigued by Carrie Chapman Catt's suggestion of the "approved suicide." First of all, it must be an act of courage and not cowardice; secondly, it involves the sort of honor of not being a burden when one's role is played out. This definition of the "approved suicide" is almost Stoic. Zeno, one of the founders of Stoicism, preached suicide to be appropriate when one's physical or mental condition prevented one from the ability to function effectively in the world and when no hope was left for improvement.

The Romans generally shared this Stoic attitude towards suicide. Pliny the Elder believed that the very existence of poisonous herbs in the world was positive proof that Divine Providence had meant for humans to be able to die quickly and painlessly when the time was right. And wise old Seneca wrote:

> I will not relinquish old age if it leaves my better part intact, but if it begins to shake my mind, if it destroys its faculties one by one, if it leaves me not life but breath, I will depart from the putrid or tottering edifice. . . . I will not raise my hand against myself on account of pain, for so to die is to be conquered. But if I know that I must suffer without hope of relief, I will depart, not through fear of pain itself, but because it prevents all for which I would live.[3]

This last statement seems immensely important. Seneca is saying that he would not kill himself because of fear of pain, since "for so to die is to be conquered." But he would kill himself if the pain kept him from "all for which I would live." This ties in directly with Carrie Chapman Catt's statement about cowardice in relation to Mrs. Gilman's suicide: "It was not cowardice as suicide is when people are afraid." There is the assertion that one must not die in fear, but rather in affirmation of one's life-full-ness and life-purpose-full-ness by attacking death before death can itself attack.

These individuals assert that there is a cowardly suicide and a courageous suicide. They insist that while any power of service remains to kill one's self on account of pain is to be conquered. But that "when all usefulness is over . . . it is the simplest of human rights to choose a quick and easy death." I imagine that Pliny the Elder would have concurred with Gilman, and would have suggested that it was for that very purpose that chloroform had been brought into the world.

But how are we to know when all usefulness is over! I know there have been times when I've felt my usefulness ended. And it is true, as James Hillman notes in *Suicide and the Soul*, that death is *not* something that comes upon us from the outside, like a thief in the night, but is that which we carry within ourselves from birth; just as we carry within us our own lives, so we carry within us our own deaths. And the recognition of that omnipresent death-within-us is a heavy burden.

You ask who is to determine "burdenness" and who is to determine "usefulness." And the terrifying question, "Should a useless person be forced to commit suicide?" My answer is an unqualified "No." As Paul Tillich says, God is not A Being, but Being Itself. Therefore, to say our lives are given by God means our lives are given by Being Itself and are part of Being Itself.

Therefore, I do not see life as having an end and a beginning, but as going on and on in some way incomprehensible to my limited intelligence. You know the old Zen koan, "What was the shape of your face before your mother conceived you?" I don't understand the mystery, but I do deeply feel that all human deaths are a part of the mainstream of life, an ongoing process, and thus must somehow be in harmony with life. Therefore, for one person to force death on another would be a violation of this principle.

It is important to remember the varying rhythms of life's movement. I remember times in my life when I have actually *done* very little (have been seen as useless), but these were really times of preparation for further doing— usefulness. Those who knew me best understood.

Remember Wordsworth's writing about the "desert

flower . . . born to bloom unseen"? That's all well and good for the desert flower! But human beings cannot exist unseen. They can exist only in relation to one another and that relating must mean action and interaction. Human beings exist only in community and that community involves giving witness to one another's being and doing. I needed my friends' understanding of my silent-preparation time. Yet had that been a permanent, not a passing place, all would have been different. You speak of society as a place for receiving others' caring as well as giving. It's true Jesus lived as a beggar in society—taking only what food and drink was offered him—not "working for a living." But he continued to give, to do, and to be. He took, only to give in return. This is very different from someone who cannot possibly give again, continuing to exist merely to take.

Recently the *New York Times* magazine section published an extraordinary letter to the editor suggesting that the "Living Will" should be extended to give persons the right not only to die rather than prolong extraordinary medical treatment, but also the right to commit suicide.[4]

The writer explained that he and his wife had long ago decided that "when we become useless in the sense of no longer being able to do our part in helping others, and therefore a burden to ourselves and those around us, we would commit suicide." He explains that his wife developed an inoperable cancer. With his full consent and cooperation, she then "in accord with a decision made a good many years ago" took an overdose. He continues, "I intend to do the same thing when I can no longer . . . do anything worthwhile, and am in danger of becoming a burden to those around me." He then tells about visiting elderly friends and relatives in nursing homes and the horror he found in the lives of those who are "vegetables in human form." (He does note that "suicide on the spur of the moment is a very different moral problem.") He continues,

"A Catholic priest who is a friend . . . told me that God has given us the gift of life; we have no right to take away that gift. I cannot believe that God has given me the gift of life to be a useless burden to others as well as to myself."

Reading this, I thought of two scenes I witnessed recently. The first was when I was having lunch with a friend at the Holiday Inn in downtown Boston (you know the place). A very old couple was sitting across from us, engaged in animated conversation, laughing and obviously enjoying one another. When they were ready to leave, the woman went to the coat rack and returned with the man's heavy steel crutches; she then helped him pull himself out of the booth, position himself on his crutches, and guided him along with an encouraging hand beneath his arm. There was great beauty there. Surely this man was no useless burden to this woman.

Then I thought of another scene I saw in the parking lot of the Coolidge Bank: a dowdy, grey-haired woman, in a housedress, physically supporting another woman who was obviously in her eighties, and obviously her mother. In the eyes of the daughter there was, as she looked at me, anxiety, despair, and a pleading for sympathy. In the eyes of the older woman, whose body was misshapen and who could barely walk, there was triumph and spite.

Now I admit this is my own script. But what I saw was an old woman, living out her days saying, "Ah ha! I've got you now! I sacrificed my life for you! Well, now it's your turn! You'll take care of *me!* Sacrifice yourself for *me!* See how *you* like it!"

There was no beauty there, my friend.

Well, I have gone on long enough for this letter.

Although I am missing Michael greatly this Thanksgiving, I am thank-full for our friendship, for being able to share, across the continent, these thoughts—even if they may not be exactly joyful. Perhaps like Dante we must make our descent into the darker regions before arising again into the light of the stars and the divine presence of "that love which moves the sun and all the stars," the presence which Dante called "God."

Where will you be for Thanksgiving? With good friends, I hope.

Write soon.

All good wishes,
Christine

REFLECTIONS

In this second exchange of letters, Rosa and Christine both express more of their personal involvement with the question of suicide, and we begin to see a polarization in their attitudes.

Rosa, contemplating the effect of her own suicide on those around her, troubled by the distractions in her life as the result of Sarah's suicide, now suggests that Sarah's suicide "might have been *ig*noble." But she doesn't say why.

She seems ambivalent in her attitude towards Charlotte Perkins Gilman's suicide, raising the question of how one's "usefulness" or "end to usefulness" is to be determined. Rosa tells of her experience with the quadriplegic woman who killed herself, and reveals the guilt she felt at that time. She now asks again if Sarah's death couldn't have been prevented. And then she presents the plea that life is to be valued *solely* as life, apart from any other criteria such as usefulness or dignity. She insists, "Our lives are somehow a gift from God."

Christine writes on two levels. On the first, she is concerned with individual losses. She is worried about Rosa's contemplation of suicide, and she is trying not to grieve over her own husband's death, which she now believes may not have been accidental. Then, on another level she writes about suicide-in-the-abstract. She discusses Vonnegut's fictional "suicide parlors" where individuals can go to have their final wishes fulfilled before ending their own lives. Finally she questions "the approved suicide," drawing distinctions between the "cowardly" and the "courageous" and between "useless" and "useful" burdens.

Separate paths in life and death are already apparent. One path is illustrated by Charlotte Perkins Gilman, who was socially oriented, really socialist in attitude. The other is illustrated by Sarah, who was individually oriented, autonomous, personal in attitude. Gilman's death was based on an idea of "the good" as "usefulness to society." Sarah's was based on "death with [personal] honor."

Gilman was a socialist, identified with the labor and woman's movements in this country at the turn of the century, a lecturer on ethics, economics, and sociology. From her first book (*Women and Economics,* 1898) to her last (*His Religion and Hers,* 1923) she insisted on the need for social reform in America. Her one novel, *What Diantha Did,* focused on the need for cooperative housekeeping among isolated women-at-home. A rebel to the end, Gilman gave directions to her daughter to have her body cremated without an undertaker's services; the request was denied by the coroner of Pasadena, California.

In failing health for several years, Gilman found even the occasion of her self-imposed death a time for crusading for a new human right—in this case, that of suicide; but only, she insisted, "when one is assured of an unavoidable and imminent death" and "when all usefulness is over"—to ensure a "quick and easy death" instead of "a slow and horrible one."

We can imagine that she might have had some quarrel with Sarah, for Gilman insists in her note that "human life consists in mutual service. No grief, pain, misfortune, or 'broken heart' is excuse for cutting off one's life while any power of service remains." Yet knowing the problems of woman's place in society, Gilman undoubtedly would have felt compassion for Sarah.

Ironically, Gilman had been given by the society which she criticized so eloquently an opportunity to use her many gifts in speaking and writing, as well as enjoying the more conventional comforts of a husband, home, and child; while Sarah, despite her parents' wealth, doubted her access to a career with an illegitimate baby, or the convenience of a conventional marriage.

Thus Sarah may well have been suffering more than Gilman, though not in pain as Gilman was. We may distinguish here between pain as physiologically based, a phenomenon which may be objectively diagnosed and either cured or treated, and suffering as a personal experience which may or may not have any physiological base. Gilman may have been in great *pain* from her cancer; but Sarah may have been *suffering* more because of her situation in society; i.e., if she had had the abortion she would be giving witness to the rightness of that deed; if she had had the baby she would have had to bear the onus of an illegitimate child.

Gilman apparently hoped her death would be a witness to others, an encouragement to break the old taboos and end one's life when the alternative was to become a useless burden. It is therefore ironic that her suicide was buried on page 44 of the *New York Times,* so that little witness effect was probably realized. (To date most suicide deaths are hidden away in the back pages of newspapers. This practice may reflect the still unacknowledged fear of this taboo subject.)

(The other side of this taboo is the idolizing of one who actually does it. This is illustrated in Sarah's case when she becomes, almost overnight, a folk heroine. She has done the unspeakable; she has committed the unpardonable.)

Rosa notes and objects to the use of the phrase "to commit suicide"—"as if it were a crime!" Historically, suicide has long been considered a crime. Until the last century in England, the bodies of suicides were desecrated by being pulled through the streets by horses. Then their corpses were buried at a crossroads with a stake through them and a stone over their faces. It was believed that these circumstances insured that the ghosts would not rise up and wander around, or, if they did, they'd either be beaten down by the traffic at the crossroads or confused as to which way to go. (It was also believed that the power of the cross itself helped purge the curse of the suicide!)

In 1823 a law was passed to abolish this custom. It was then decreed that burial was to be private, at night, and without religious rites. By 1882 suicides were at last allowed to be buried during the day, but the official Church of England service still could not be officially used.

In America, it was Massachusetts which first imported this practice of "unholy internment." In 1660 the Massachusetts legislature announced that it "judgeth that God calls them to bear testimony against such wicked and unnatural practices, that others may be deterred therefrom." Therefore, they decreed that every suicide "shall be buried in some common highway where the selectmen of the town where such person did inhabit shall appoint, and a cartload of stones laid upon the grave, as a brand of infamy, and as a warning to others to beware of the like damnable practices."

Why such fear? Why should the bodies of those who chose to end their lives be treated with such abuse and anger?

Part of the fear was surely that of the fear of death itself. But none of the four Old Testament suicides recorded, that of Samson, who killed himself and the Philistines by pulling down the pillars of the temple (Judg. 16:28–31); Saul, who slew himself after defeat in battle to avoid the shame of capture (1 Sam. 31:1–6); Abimelech, who killed himself after being fatally wounded by a woman so it could not be said he had been killed by a woman (Judg. 9:54); and Ahitophel, who hung himself when he betrayed David to

Absalom (2 Sam. 17:23), none of these men are condemned. And, despite condemnation of the act by the Jewish law, there have been instances in Jewish history of mass suicide which have been praised—the most famous example being, perhaps, that of the Zealots who took refuge in Masada to avoid capture by their enemies; when capture was inevitable, Eleazar Ben Jair urged his followers to kill themselves rather than fall into the enemy's hands. They did.

In ancient Greek and Roman times, suicides were condoned for the following reasons—to show bereavement, to preserve honor, to avoid pain and shame, and for the benefit of the state. The philosophies of the Cynics, the Stoics, and the Epicureans accepted suicide. Pythagoras opposed it, believing that a suicide upset the "spiritual mathematics" of the world. Aristotle condemned it as an act against the state. Plato, in his *Phaedo,* has Socrates say that suicide is permissible in cases of incurable illness or when God has summoned the soul; but, in general, since man is the property and "the soldier" of the gods, suicide is tantamount to desertion.

Until A.D. 250, suicide was common among the early Christians. They wanted to "go home to meet their Maker" and be with Christ. There were many martyrs who sought their own deaths. Three types of suicide were especially common—voluntary martyrdom, the death of the virgin or married woman to preserve chastity, and the self-inflicted death (often by starvation) of the ascetic. But when it became clear that the Second Coming was not immediately at hand, and that the Church was going to have to abide for a while as an earthly institution, prohibitions against suicide became strict.

Augustine began to codify these prohibitions in his *City of God* (ca. A.D. 410). He based his condemnation on the sixth commandment—"Thou shalt not kill." He insisted that suicide was murder, that the suicidee was the worst of sinners because he surrendered any hope of absolution, and that the truly noble soul would bear all suffering rather than try to escape through self-inflicted death.

The Council of Arles (A.D. 452) condemned the suicide of servants *(famuli)* because of the repercussions on the master and landowner. So the first official Church condemnation was over a matter of human property and the rights of the survivors. In A.D. 533, the Second Council of Orleans ruled that the Church could receive offerings of those who were killed committing a crime, but not of those who killed themselves. In A.D. 563 the Council of Braga denied the suicide regular funeral rites, and the Synod of Nimes in 1284 refused burial in holy ground to suicides. Then began the custom of desecrating the corpse by dragging it through the streets and burying it at a crossroads.

Writing in the thirteenth century, Thomas Aquinas formulated the official church position for that time. In his *Summa Theologica* he stated that suicide was wrong because: (1) it was unnatural; (2) it was antisocial; (3) life was a gift of God and not at the disposal of the individual.

But then came the Renaissance and the Reformation with new emphasis on the importance of the individual, and attitudes once again began to change. The poet John Donne wrote the first defense of suicide in the English language in his essay "Bianthanatos," published posthumously in 1644; it declared that circumstances alter the conditions of suicides and thus each must be judged individually. It is possible that Shakespeare also contributed to a more general acceptance of suicide; in his eight tragedies there are fourteen suicides; and such characters as Hamlet and King Lear probe the attraction which the deed has for the sensitive individual.

David Hume's "On Suicide" (also published posthumously in 1783) argued that: (1) suicide was not a crime against God because God gave the individual the power to act, and therefore death at one's own hands was as much under God's control as any other death; (2) suicide was not a crime against society for one who takes his own life does no harm to others, but only ceases to do good, and if that is a wrong, it is of the lowest kind; (3) suicide is not a crime against the self because no one ever throws away a life worth the keeping.

So attitudes were changing by the end of the eighteenth century. A Frenchman named Merian published a tract in 1763 arguing that suicide was an illness, not a crime. Thus "suicide while of unsound mind" became an acceptable means of avoiding Church disapproval. Still today a suicide may receive proper burial if the act is believed not to have been done thoughtfully and rationally, but in a moment of madness.

In 1885 a man named Thomas Bonser published a short paper in London called *The right to die*, arguing that the state has no right to interfere with an individual's suicide. The right to suicide, he argued, was not one granted by society and therefore could not be rescinded by society.

With the publication of Emile Durkheim's classic *Le Suicide* in 1897, suicide entered the realm of scientific study. Durkheim's sociological study claimed, essentially, that where social solidarity was strong, there would be little suicide; where it was weak, there would be more. And in the twentieth century, the study of suicide was given over principally to the psychologists—the best known being Norman Faberow and Edwin Schneidman. The modern theologians, with few exceptions, have been strangely silent on the matter.[5]

As Rosa notes, the phrase "to commit" suicide connotes a crime. But perhaps we can reconsider this meaning. "To commit" may mean "to do" or "to perform" as in "to commit a crime." But it may also mean "to give in trust or charge; to entrust; to consign; to commend; to hand over for treatment or for safekeeping" as in "to commit one's soul to God."

If this latter connotation were put upon the phrase, surely a different social attitude would begin to prevail. Christine suggests this possibility when she writes of our lives being "part of Being Itself" and thus "going on and on in some way incomprehensible to my limited intelligence." She is speaking here of God as being not A Being, but Being Itself (a concept of the late theologian, Paul Tillich) and thus our lives as a gift from Being Itself which can never be rescinded, not even by death. This seems close to Paul's declaration in his epistle to the Romans (14:8), "If we live, we live to the Lord, and if we die, we die to the Lord; so then, whether we live or whether we die, we are the Lord's."

Whether or not suicide is a crime may easily be decided by checking the legislation on the books in whatever judicial province the act takes place. (Only seven of America's fifty states currently retain laws against attempted suicide; eighteen have laws against aiding and abetting a suicide.) Whether or not suicide is a "sin," i.e., a transgression of divine law which leads to separation from God, is another matter, a question which neither Christine nor Rosa have yet asked.

CHAPTER 3

HEMINGWAY: *A Time to Die*

Hanukkah
Berkeley

Dear Christine,

Please don't worry, My suicide imaginings are just imaginings—probably prompted by all the time I spend with the planning committee for the Suicide Prevention Center. I'm okay.

How are you? I know how difficult it must have been for you to make Thanksgiving dinner for yourself without Michael to share it, but perhaps doing it in memory of him was one way of "kindling the lights" in his absence, symbolizing the love you shared.

Today is Hanukkah. I'll be attending the celebration with a Jewish friend—a first for me—and will say a prayer for you during the lighting of the candles. And of course, one for Sarah.

Christine, I was intrigued with what you said about Charlotte Gilman's suicide—that it had an element of witness in it because it was done as an act of social service. I've never thought of suicide as a way of witnessing before, but perhaps it can be! She believed only usefulness was important. But is that any kind of model for what could be considered an "acceptable" or "justifiable" suicide? You seem to say yes, but I'm not at all sure. What *is* a good basis for killing oneself?

At this point I see suicide as an act of last resort. We live in an unjust society. Fate is unjust, and so is suffering. But does that make suicide permissible?

You mentioned Seneca, and I agree with him that there's no good to be found in suffering as suffering. But Christine, I've observed in my own life and others' that suffering is only *one* of the many varieties of human condition, like the feeling of uselessness or loss of honor. I don't affirm suffering under any circumstances, but I don't agree with Seneca that it is the basis of a *right* to take one's own life. If suicide is to be thought of as an *innate human right* I think it must be based on something more all-inclusive than suffering.

What about Hemingway? (I didn't realize Hemingway's father had committed suicide! Yet I must have read it somewhere.) I remember vividly how shocked I was when I read of Hemingway's death. It was a bright July morning in the Midwest. And by coincidence I'd been going through a Hemingway phase, reading one novel after another. I escaped my hospital work and became everything in his books I'm not in real life! An adventurer, world traveler, revolutionary. I cooked over an open fire in the Spanish highlands and slept in a cave; I hiked in the African bush country, and climbed Kilamanjaro! When Hemingway died that morning, in his own home with his wife upstairs, it was reported as an accident. But I think everybody knew better.

Christine, it was a whole year before I got over the feeling that Hemingway had somehow betrayed me by dying before he wrote more books. Certainly, to offer any *one* explanation about why Hemingway shot himself, such as his father's suicide, is to do a complex person and a great writer an injustice. Was it the last potent act left to him in his failing health?

Or do you think he himself would interpret his suicide as an existentially positive act? His final way of showing that life, both physical and creative, is the ultimate irony because it ends in death?

Didn't Camus, Sartre, and other such existentialist writers view life as an absurdity? It was Hemingway who reminded us that we are, each of us, an old man fighting the sea in order, at last, only to make it to shore with the skeleton of our life. Those who hold illusions of life being more are eventually crucified upon the eternal question mark. And Hemingway may have thought that it was best to meet Death on his own terms, rather than to let It set the conditions. If so, he would be like the Stoics who saw the importance of dying *well,* courageously, at the right moment.

But this raises another kind of question. Does it really matter if a person (Hemingway, Charlotte Gilman) who kills him or herself is courageous? Does the motive make a significant difference? If I promise something to you, does it matter in the end if I keep my promise with great courage or creeping cowardice? The motive might make some difference in what you think of ME, but little bearing on whether I kept my promise. So I fail to see that the *act* of suicide is altered by the person's motive.

Christine, I don't see death as an enemy to be conquered courageously. I don't want to "attack death before it can attack me." It is less important for me to feel I'm in control than it was for Seneca and the Stoics because I've observed/felt that the life-full-ness and life-purpose-full-ness (those are marvelous words you chose!) are often discovered at the breaking points, rather than when I am in control in the rational way of the Stoics. My own life-heartedness has been realized at those times of personal loss, pain, or other kinds of suffering; and also when I've lost touch with solid ground during periods of exceeding joy! At the moments of losing life I have found it. I have not been conquered by these little deaths, nor did my courage save me. I think the dignity attached to being in control describes the machismo ethic which Hemingway lived and wrote about, and is really no justification for suicide.

Finally, Christine, I've been thinking about Hemingway as an *artist*. Why do many artists of all types kill themselves? Must they all *test* death from time to time, the way that Sylvia Plath seems to have done, to prove they are alive? Do they feel that their self-inflicted death is a truly creative act?

Actually, now that I can remember it without too much pain there was a strong element of drama in Sarah's suicide! She arranged the stage and the props with great care. The typewriter, the note. She chose to wear her lavender satin robe, and let her freshly combed hair flow over her pillow. The timing was perfect. (She knew we would all be there on Saturday morning.) I'm obviously not as detached from the scene as I sound, but I know a lot of aesthetic planning went into her act! Suicide having an artistic element? Just maybe . . .

Must write to Mother now. She is fussing again—why don't I get married and settle down, etc., etc.? I'm now twice an aunt, thanks to my younger sister. (Mom never bothers my brother about getting married.)

I'm already looking forward to your next letter. Til then.

Adieu,
Rosa

Dear Rosa,

This is in lieu of a Christmas card. I'm not celebrating the holidays this year (with both Mother and Michael gone, Christmas isn't the same). But I'm taking the time to write to a few special friends.

I'm writing to you first because I'm still concerned with your preoccupation with your own suicidal thoughts. Are you getting professional help? I trust you are.

Christmas.

Christ's mass.

Do you remember the Christmas Eve we went to midnight mass at Per L'Universo Church off Columbus Street in San Francisco? Do you remember all the Christmas Eve services you must have gone to when you were growing up—sharing them with your older brother who teased you and your baby sister? Don't we all wish at Christmas that we could be children again? Children not faced with the sorts of problems that you and I have been dealing with in our letters?

But that, of course, is just another illusion—the myth of the happy childhood when all the world was filled with tinsel. Which of us, in our early days, has not been faced with the very sorts of problems we've been discussing in our letters? Problems of life, of love, of death. Hemingway, for example. Surely one of the strongest memories he carried with him of his childhood was of his father's suicide. Can you imagine the scene? Ernest's father, the good doctor who saved lives, who brought new lives into the world, this man putting a gun to his own head and pulling the trigger when Ernest was still a boy?

How much of the memory was with Ernest that July day he ended his own life? In how many ways did he see his killing of himself to be the proper ending of his own life-script, his last truly creative act? And can we blame his wife, "Miss Mary," for originally trying to deny the reality of his suicide when she told the press it had all been an accident, a slip of the hand while he was cleaning his gun?[1] (Certainly, it wasn't the way *she* would have written the script.) But Hemingway, consummate artist that he was, managed to keep control of the final scene. . . .

The denial of the purpose and of the purposefulness of the deed and of the death. Yet there is no such denial in the words of Tennessee Williams, who in eulogizing Hemingway made a most moving statement of the relation between Hemingway's work and his death. He said,

> Hemingway knew that an artist's work, the heart of it, is finally himself and his life, and he accomplished, as few artists that have lived in our time, if any, the almost impossibly difficult achievement of becoming, as a man, in the sight of the world and the time he lived in, the embodiment of what his work meant, on its highest and most honest level, and it would seem that he continued this achievement until the moment of death, which he would undoubtedly call his "moment of truth," in all truth.[2]

I don't think Tennessee Williams considers himself an existentialist, any more than Hemingway would have accepted that label. Yet this emphasis on the moment of truth being the moment in which we face death is at the core of the existentialist writings.

You remember Camus's writing that "there is but one truly serious philosophical problem, and that is suicide"? I'm beginning to understand what he meant—that the most fundamental choice which we all make is whether or not to live. I've never really thought about this before, so the realization comes as an epiphany to me. If I didn't have the possibility of suicide, life would be intolerable! That is, if I didn't have the belief that I could choose my own exit line from this play of life, if I believed I might have to go on and on till Someone Else pushed me off stage, I would feel helpless and futile. Life would be a prison. Choice is truly the epitome and essence of my free choice as a human being. It's what sets me apart as a human being from the rest of nature.

Sartre distinguishes between *l'être-pour-soi* (being-for-itself) and *l'être-en-soi* (being-in-itself). If a person chooses to escape the responsibility of human freedom, then that individual has chosen to escape into the object world of *l'être-en-soi*, has become less than human, and thus is living in bad faith *(la mauvaise foi)* with the world. And one of the greatest decisions which any individual is faced with is how or when to die in *good* faith.

I am now beginning to understand the idea of "the moment of truth" when one is closest to death and all side issues fall away. One side issue is that of pain. Hemingway wrote once of a bullfighter he admired greatly—Maera. Maera had a fatal illness, yet continued to fight. One Sunday afternoon Hemingway saw him fight with a five-inch, two-day-old wound in his armpit—"He paid no attention to the pain," Hemingway wrote; "he acted as though it were not there. He did not favor it or avoid lifting the arm; he ignored it. He was a long way beyond pain."

Again we see the value of one living in pain; of pain itself not being a reason for dying. If pain is not important, in this existentialist ethic, what is? A code of living, a style of life that involves pride, dignity, defiance, and honor?

In Hemingway's brief scenario "Today is Friday," his

telling of the Good Friday story, the first soldier says of Jesus, "He was pretty good in there today." What is to be admired is the bearing up under pressure; grace under pressure; even the pressure unto death. Death with honor. So Santiago in *The Old Man and the Sea* "knew he was beaten now finally and without remedy." He had gone out too far, but he would go out again and again, until his death. And when he could no longer go out he would die, for there is that need in him as there was in his creator, Hemingway, to always be living on the borderline of physical risk. Hemingway wrote of himself in *Portraits and Self-Portraits:*

> Since he was a young boy he has cared greatly for fishing and shooting. If he had not spent so much time at them . . . he might have written much more. On the other hand, he might have shot himself.[3]

You write, Rosa, that you were angry with Hemingway for killing himself when he could have written more books for you to read. But this quote and his whole life seem to indicate that like Santiago, when he could no longer go out to lead a physically active life and when he felt his writing powers fail him, he could no longer live. For him to *be* was to *be-in-action,* and write. He did not wish to continue to exist as a primarily passive object on which tests were taken and to which medicine and treatments were given (*l'être-en-soi*).

I believe that on that early Sunday morning when he went down from his bedroom in his pajamas to sit in the hallway chair and pull the trigger of the shotgun pointed in his mouth, he was thinking. "I am sick and deteriorating. Soon they will want to keep me in the hospital all the time. I can't live or die like that."

And so he pulled the trigger.

You say that you believe Hemingway's need to be in control is more a reflection of his machismo ethic than it is any real basis for judging whether or not a person is justified in taking his or her own life. And you write of the times in your own life as being replete with life-full-ness and life-purposeful-ness when you were least in control. Isn't it all in the individual? What if Hemingway had chosen to live on (to use a phrase we both hate) as a vegetable? It's one thing to die quickly or to be killed. It's something else to have it happen while your physical and mental strengths weaken and fail. Perhaps he imagined an occasional newspaper picture of the sickly Hemingway, the aging Hemingway, the Hemingway who could no longer even hold a shotgun, let alone go out hunting with it! Could he have kept his dignity through that?

You seem to imply that dignity is a quality given freely and equally to all along with life. I disagree. Dignity is given almost by grace. It's a differentiating quality, a matter of degree. Everyone has dignity, but some have more than others! And some care about it more than others.

But excuse me, my friend! On Christmas Eve to get so carried away! Yet, still, I must reply to your questions.

You also raise the question of the role of motive. As long as the act is done, does it matter what the motives are? My answer is: Yes, very much. There is a great deal of difference between the individual who takes his or her own life as an act of despair and hopelessness, or as a way of getting back at someone else, or as a negation of all the life that has been led previously and as a means of injuring the community; and the individual who takes his or her life as an act of affirmation and hope, as a way of saving useless pain and trouble to loved ones, and as a way of helping the community, as a yea-saying to all.

Rosa, I can't see Sarah's death as yea-saying. But certainly Charlotte Gilman's was positive. And possibly Hemingway's.

To me the individual life is not a gift, but a loan. We use

it as best we can for as long as we can—fruitfully, productively, and well—and then we offer it back to the loan-giver. To carry the metaphor further, when it seems to any one of us that we're no longer gaining interest on our loan of life, then is the time to give back what we have been given, leaving the world, Life Itself, no less and no worse for our having been.

I believe that an individual's life is the result of a compact or a covenant, or if you will a loan agreement between that individual and God. (And secondarily, to the extent that person wills, between the individual and his or her community.) I believe suicide to be the right of response-able individuals. That is, individuals able and willing to respond rationally and sensitively to the world around them. When one is no longer response-able, then one cannot choose. Thus I would never advise suicide to the individual deeply despondent after the death of a loved one, or after some other catastrophe, such as the loss of a limb or the loss of one's sight. Suicide should be chosen by a person who is response-able to make other choices too—otherwise the concept of choice means nothing and the dignity of choice is lost.

I'm guessing, of course, but maybe some artists need to choose their deaths, to create them according to some plan of their own, to kill themselves off as they have killed off the characters they have written about—to not leave their own endings to chance any more than the endings of any of the characters in their works. For the true artist is always first and foremost a creator. And in that sense he or she is godlike; the creator of a unique universe. Therefore it may be natural, as you suggest in your letter, for artists, writers especially, to feel they are the potential creators and destroyers of themselves as well as of the characters they create.

Read Sylvia Plath's *Letters Home* and her novel, *The Bell Jar.*

Both books describe her suicide attempts. Sylvia's drive to death did not have to do with the loss of her creative power or an end to social usefulness. What it did have to do with, I can only intimate from her poetry—lines like these:

> Dying
> Is an art, like everything else,
> I do it exceptionally well.
>
> I do it so it feels like hell.
> I do it so it feels real.
> I guess you could say I've a call.[4]

Or from her poem, "Edge," which again expresses the need to have it all end well, according to some sort of self-imposed schedule. She wrote these lines shortly before her suicide:

> The woman is perfected,
> Her dead
>
> Body wears the smile of accomplishment,
> The illusion of a Greek Necessity
>
> Flows in the scrolls of her toga,
> Her bare
>
> Feet seem to be saying:
> We have come so far, it is over.[5]

In this second poem I do have the feeling of the planned death being a sort of "Amen, so let it be," spoken to the life lived. But perhaps that is just the literary me—the part that says, yes, of course, it had to be that Jocasta killed herself after discovering she was the mother of Oedipus, her husband-son. Or the part that says yes and amen to Romeo's killing himself for Juliet, and then Juliet in turn killing herself because Romeo was dead. Or the part that says amen to Antigone's hanging herself and Haemon's stabbing herself in her cave-tomb, or to Antony and Cleopatra's each committing suicide rather than yielding to the victory of the cold Roman emperor Octavian.

I can see that our discussion is going to keep expanding as our questions grow and answers appear, only to disappear. This suicide discussion is a lot more complex than I had thought it would be! Perhaps the way to end this letter is with a quote from Euripides, who ended several of his plays with it.

> There be many shapes of mystery
> And many things God makes to be,
>   Past hope or fear.
> And the end men looked for cometh not,
> And a path is there where no man thought . . .
>   So hath it fallen here.[6]

I'm wondering where you are this Christmas Eve. Here there is snow and cold. Tonight at David's we'll have a fire and probably even roast chestnuts! Have you gone home to your family for Christmas?

I've just tried to call you. No answer. I'll try again tomorrow, just to wish you a happy holiday. Meanwhile, know that you'll be in my prayers tonight as I go to the midnight service at Old Cambridge Baptist.

Surely these Holidays cannot last much longer.

If I miss you tomorrow (the circuits are always crowded Christmas Day), call me anytime, collect if you wish.

Christine

P.S. I'll be gone the last two weeks in January—off to St. Thomas at the semester break to try and get some writing done and to lift my spirits in the sun. Address there is enclosed.

REFLECTIONS

IN THIS exchange of letters, Rosa and Christine are both more personal and also more abstract (dealing with the questions of rights, of dignity, and of control) in their attitude toward suicide.

Hemingway's suicide leads them to very different conclusions. To Rosa such a desire to maintain control right up to the moment of death itself is based on some kind of machismo ethic which sees control as the one great good, an ethic in which an individual, in order to maintain control, may kill him or herself.

Christine on the other hand sees this need to control one's dying as permissible if not laudable. But she admits that she may be the victim of what Sylvia Plath called "the illusion of a Greek Necessity."

A central issue involved is one of rights. The question really asked is, "Does an individual have a *right* to commit suicide?" (They still have not directly asked the question, "Is suicide a *sin?*")

The question of human rights has been at the center of law and government for centuries. The French revolution was based on the claim that all persons had a right to liberty, fraternity, and equality. The American revolution claimed that all had the rights of life, liberty, and the pursuit of happiness (although actually "all" was interpreted to mean only white-skinned adult males).

The nineteenth-century British philosopher, John Stuart

Mill, defined a right as "an innate human quality which should not be interfered with." He allowed that the only time a person could be constrained from exercising a right was if the person was impinging on another person's rights.

Recently, the U.S. Supreme Court ruled an important new right: the right to privacy (*Griswold et al.* vs. *Conn.*, 1965) thereby creating the basis for a number of significant new legislative decisions, including the 1973 decision legalizing abortion.

Today in America a person need only be a human being in order to have certain rights. One does not earn a right, and theoretically and technically at least cannot lose it by giving it away. For instance, in the U.S., one cannot legally enter into a slavery agreement. Thus the state can intervene if a person seems to be acting in poor judgment, contrary to protecting his or her own human rights, as surely as if he or she were impinging on someone else's. This right of the state to protect the person from his or her own poor judgment has led to such practices as compulsory vaccination, compulsory sterilization, and involuntary commission to mental institutions.

Now any lasting change in public attitudes regarding suicide will depend at least in part upon whether the majority of people agree that choosing their own manner and time of death is a basic human right. Our society bases many of its mores and most of its laws on this underriding notion of rights, whether or not the word *right* is actually used.

Decidedly, in America (as opposed to say Sweden), the prevailing notion towards suicide is that it is not a human right. Its long history of being considered legally a crime, the indignities heaped upon suicide corpses, and the penalties suffered by the survivors of a suicide have long suggested that it was an act to be guarded against. Today suicide prevention centers, heroic last-minute attempts to dissuade persons from taking their own lives, and the stigma attached to those who commit suicide are indicators that this attitude still persists.

But a countercurrent is being heard, too. It finds its strongest support among those who propose that a person has a right to "die with dignity." Appalled by the treatment of persons in the final stages of terminal illness, or of others who are suffering, the proponents of this view cry for acknowledgement that physical life should not be preserved *at all costs.* They maintain that if a right to die with dignity were legalized, then the attitudes of society toward suicide would eventually change—less stigma would be attached to it and more support would attend the person contemplating it. These persons like Christine are essentially appealing to the individual's ability to decide when and how one will die.

Rosa is opposed to this position because she believes that life itself is the supreme value—not control, not freedom from suffering, not usefulness. She insists that human life is not proportional to the sum of its merits, and the taking of a human life cannot be justified because of the lack of any particular qualities of that life. She insists that the intrinsic value of a person's life is attached to something over and above the individual's merit. She remains convinced that life is of itself a supreme value and must not be violated by self-inflicted death.

In general, the contrast between the two positions may be put thusly: Christine argues the existentialist position: she believes that every "response-able" person has the right to make his/her decision about suicide. Thus the burden of proof lies on the individual who is trying to *dissuade* a person from suicide. Rosa believes that the right-to-the-sustenance-of-life is the moral law, and that the burden of proof lies on the person who *wants* to die a self-inflicted death. Suicide is not viewed as a right in itself.

Christine's existential argument is based on the belief

that choice is of the essence of humanity and the most important choice a human can make is whether or not to live. It is this ability *to choose* which differentiates human life from other forms of life. Her analysis is akin to that of Martin Heidegger, one of Sartre's mentors in philosophy, who describes the passive state of natural objects, i.e., objects in nature, as *Vorhandenheit* ("being-in-itself") as opposed to the active state of human life lived with integrity and authenticity which he calls *Dasein* ("being-for-itself"). To Heidegger, the individual who lives purposefully as *Dasein* is the truly authentic individual.

This description by the German atheist-existentialist is amazingly close to one of the most ardent Christian thinkers and writers of our time, that of the German theologian and martyr Dietrich Bonhoeffer. In Bonhoeffer's *Ethics* (published posthumously), he distinguishes man from the beasts in this way:

> Man, unlike the beasts, does not carry his life as a compulsion which he cannot throw off. He is free either to accept his life or to destroy it. Unlike the beasts man can put himself to death of his own free will. An animal is one with the life of his body, but man can distinguish himself from the life of his body. The freedom in which man possesses his bodily life requires him to accept this life freely, and at the same time it directs his attention to what lies beyond this bodily life and compels him to regard the life of his body as a gift that is to be preserved and a sacrifice that is to be offered. Only because a man is free to choose death can he lay down the life of his body for some higher good. Without freedom to sacrifice one's life in death, there can be no freedom towards God, there can be no human life.[7]

Christine says, "If I didn't have the possibility of suicide, life would be intolerable!"

The previous Reflections suggested that the concept of suicide might be changed if the verb *commit* were to be thought of as "to give in trust or charge; to entrust" (as in "to commit one's soul to God") rather than "to do" (as in "to commit a crime"). This concept tends to elevate the act to that of sacrifice—offering up one's life to God—not the taking of a life, but the giving of a life. Bonhoeffer, similarly, shows the relation of suicide to sacrifice.

Bonhoeffer sharply distinguishes suicide done out of fear, disappointment in love, or personal dishonor from suicide done not for personal reasons, but for a cause. When he speaks of "the liberty and the right to death," he is speaking of suicide as surrendering life for a good which is higher than the value of the bodily life, i.e., a cause which would be related to one's discipleship to God.

It is not likely that Bonhoeffer would have condoned Hemingway's suicide. Yet he writes with understanding of the act in words which could be applied to Hemingway:

> Suicide is a man's attempt to give a final human meaning to a life which has become humanly meaningless. The involuntary sense of horror which seizes us when we are faced with the fact of a suicide is not to be attributed to the iniquity of such a deed but to the terrible loneliness and freedom in which this deed is performed, a deed in which the positive attitude to life is reflected only in the destruction of life.[8]

Bonhoeffer's attitude here is akin to Christine's insistence on the difference between a suicide done as "an act of despair and hopelessness . . . a negation of all the life that has been," and a suicide done as "an act of affirmation and hope . . . as a yea-saying to all that has been, with this act as the final 'Yea! Amen! So let it be!' " The latter may be seen as "a deed in which the positive attitude to life is reflected only in the destruction of life," in the words of Bonhoeffer quoted above.

This presupposes an ideal of choosing an end to life rather than living out a biological existence void of meaningful action. Such an ideal is based on the belief that the human being is a historical being and that his or her being-as-such is validated primarily by his or her actively being-in-the-world.

Of course, there are many ways of being-in-the-world other than the sort of *machismo* manner in which Hemingway lived. Hemingway was in the tradition of the Great American Hero. It is a tradition in which potency and manhood are shown through use of the symbolic gun or sword—the soldier, the bullfighter, and the hunter—these are the Hemingway heroes—all killers.

Is it possible that Hemingway not only lived and created this script in his novels, but also eventually fell victim to it? When he could no longer be potent, i.e., potent-ially the killer, and the writer-killer, he had to kill the last thing left —himself, the artist. So he became, in one sense, his own victim—or the victim of the myth.

Hemingway was living by a stereotypically male-oriented myth. (His is not a mystique for most women.) And it is possible that had he been able to change scripts—to find another way-of-being-in-the-world, he could have continued to live meaningfully. In the next exchange of letters, we will find Rosa and Christine discussing Marilyn Monroe, the victim of the super-female stereotype, just as Hemingway was the victim of the super-male stereotype. Ernest Hemingway and Marilyn Monroe both came to the end of their ability or to the end of their desire to play their stereotyped roles. They were both unable, for various reasons, to successfully write for themselves another script. And (we can surmise) they both chose death rather than to become parodies of their former selves.

Christine writes of the right to suicide when one can no longer "preserve one's own way of being in the world." What she does not consider is the possibility of finding another way of being. This is the option many individuals face when suddenly they have lost a limb or an organ or the ability to speak or see or walk. These individuals must either find another way of being in the world or cease to be. (The only other alternative is to negate and deny their present reality.) It takes bravery and slow, patient determination to find another way of being. Many do not. They may wither away slowly or end their lives quickly. How are we to judge them?

Bonhoeffer again emphasizes the importance of the *motive*. He says that the right to live is conditional upon freedom, and then offers the very exciting idea that "the right to live has as its counterpart the freedom to offer and to give one's life in sacrifice."[9] This statement implies again what Christine was suggesting—that truly authentic human life exists only as it is purposefully *chosen*—and must always carry with it the possibility of choosing *death* instead. But Bonhoeffer does not speak just of choosing death, rather very specifically of offering and giving one's life in sacrifice. He insists that "man possesses the liberty and the right to death, but only so long as his purpose in risking and surrendering his life is not the destruction of his life but the good for the sake of which he offers this sacrifice."[10] Again, we find the insistence that one must offer one's life for some higher good to meet the conditions of the approved suicide/death.

Bonhoeffer believes that man can easily abuse his liberty to die. In fact, "he can by his own free decision seek death in order to avoid defeat and he may thus rob fate of its victory."[11] On the other hand, he says that "it cannot be contested that through this deed a man is once again asserting his manhood, even though he may be misunderstanding its significance, and that he is opposing it effectively to the blind inhuman force of destiny."[12]

This latter sentence could almost be an existentialist's commentary on *The Old Man and the Sea*. Santiago, the old man, may be seen as the hero who does "assert his manhood" even against "the blind inhuman force of destiny" which he meets in the form of the sharks at sea. Bonhoeffer sees such suicidal behavior as wrong, though understandable, because the individual (whom, to Bonhoeffer, is always "man") is thus trying to "rob fate of its victory." But Christine suggests that perhaps such a death may, in itself, be part of "the victory of fate."

She implies the possibility that the heroes and heroines of Greek tragedy who died self-inflicted deaths actually did so not in spite of, but in light of, some powers of fate which other mortals could not see. Consider the classical case in which Oedipus and Jocasta were bound in a web of fate which seemed, of necessity, to lead to Jocasta's suicide and to Oedipus' self-blinding (the extreme sort of self-mutilation which may be seen to be a sort of suicide). Or consider Antigone, who because she obeyed the commandments of the gods instead of the king's edict found herself imprisoned in a cave from which to her knowledge there was to be no escape. She hanged herself rather than suffer slow starvation. It seems part of the fate of this noble woman that she did this brave deed (following her other brave deeds) before she could be rescued by her beloved Haemon. Had she been truly rescued there would have been no play, *Antigone.* It was not only that she was willing to risk death, but that she did indeed die that made her a heroine.

One more word about the heroic suicide—a final point about Bonhoeffer's conception of the right to die. He does not condone all suicide, but he does believe that "the ultimate right to dispose of himself . . . is conferred on a man [*sic*] by nature."[13] Thus he disagrees with Aquinas who believes that the human does not have the right to decide how to dispose of his/her own life. Bonhoeffer insists that "the community may impose penalties on a suicide, but it will not be able to convince the offender himself that it possesses a valid right over his life." To this theologian the question is not one of the state's right, but one, very truly, of sin. The subject of sin will unfold in some of the following Reflections. Bonhoeffer believes, "If this action [suicide] is performed in freedom it is raised high above any petty moralizing accusation of cowardice and weakness." [14] What does it mean for one to die in freedom? What does it mean for one to die in sin?

CHAPTER 4

MARILYN MONROE:
Let Him Who Is Without Sin

3 January
Berkeley

Dear Christine,

Happy New Year!

But what, I wonder, is really new about it? It's curious: we hold the illusion that hope springs from the decaying last days of December. We greet the new year with such promises! We believe in the "new leaf!"

Oh! I'm not in much of a gala New Year mood, and it's not because of too much partying either. I guess it's because most of the students have gone home for Christmas vacation. The corridors of the dorm seem twice as wide; my footsteps echo; and the heat's been turned down so that I have to wear a coat just to go to the kitchen. I'm feeling really lonely and depressed, as if this space/time will never end. (No, I didn't go home for Christmas—couldn't afford it.)

Last night I had a strange dream, another one about Sarah. I dreamed that I was in a room much like this dorm room, lying on a narrow little cot. I was in a half slumber, snuggled under some heavy blankets, when I felt a chilling breeze swooping back and forth over my head. I opened my eyes. There were four or five huge translucent forms, something like bats flying overhead, and I knew they were the proverbial angels of death. I kicked out at them, but my blanketed foot went right through their ghostlike bodies. Then I yelled, "NO! NO! Don't come at me. I'm all alone!" Just then I looked over and saw Sarah. She was in a little bed on the other side of the room. In fact there were several beds with people in them. She raised up on her elbow and said, "It's OK . . . I'm here." Today the depression that followed the dream has settled on me like one of those bats. It's a cold, heavy, suffocating feeling, and I can't get away from it. It's really scaring me because the one time in my life I seriously thought of committing suicide, I had the feeling I have now. It's a feeling of the world narrowing down to only my small capsule of life.

You never met Paul. Sometimes I wish I had never met him either. But Paul touched me more deeply than any other living human being. We really loved each other, but all we ever did was hurt each other. I know now that it couldn't have worked; we lived in different worlds and we differed on some of the most basic values. (Mom and Dad both told me so.) But I wanted desperately for it to work. And when it began crumbling, so did I. One night we both cried like little kids, held each other, knowing it wasn't going to work, afraid to take the next step. I finally did it— left his apartment. He had prepared dinner but we never ate it. I remember the way the table looked. I took an olive on my way out and when I had been walking blindly up and down the streets of San Francisco for several hours, I realized I still had that olive pit between my teeth. I cried torrents. I can't remember how I got home or when. All I know is that I woke up the next afternoon about three o'clock. I decided to take an overdose. You know, Christine, I *would* have if Delores hadn't just happened to have stopped by unexpectedly.

That night from the time I left his apartment until the next day when Delores came I felt totally lost; there was no past, present, or future; no outdoors, no movement of the stars, no sidewalks, no trees, no people. Only the relationship.

You know we've never talked about this before, but have you ever considered committing suicide? Or tried it? I wonder what makes someone like Sarah actually go ahead with it? Why some of us just think about it, and others actually *do* it.

Damn Sarah! I've really been missing her recently. I thought I had worked through my feelings about her death, but lately I've been mourning her all over again. I miss her spunkiness—her impulsiveness—the sound of her records coming under the door. I miss her teasing. I miss my family too I guess! I miss *you* off in the Caribbean!

Christine, what a surprising woman you are! You write on and on about Greek literary heroines while my thoughts have been turning to Marilyn Monroe! I remember what Marilyn Monroe meant to my family and me. My mother looked down on her as a wicked woman on screen and off. Dad acted as though he agreed. I was a scrawny, clumsy teenager with mousy brown hair and I couldn't identify with her at all. She was a movie star seductress, not a woman. So I wasn't in the least moved by the news of her overdose back in 1962. There had been reports of her increasing legal entanglements, her divorce from Arthur Miller. I'm ashamed to admit it now, but I may have felt some kind of satisfaction that she (whom we felt had everything) had been brought down from her pinnacle. I felt detached. She had never really lived for me, and so it was impossible for me to feel that she had really died. The legend she inspired almost completely wiped out any clear picture of who she was (or wasn't), what she felt, and why she may have died.

Now you've started me thinking—and reading. Of all the books on MM, the one I'm most impressed by is *Norma Jean* by Fred Guiles. Have you read it? Guiles helped me believe that MM was once a little girl like me, that she had a brother like mine and that they fought, and that she sang "Jesus Loves Me" in Sunday School the way I did. I began to visualize Norma Jean turned screen star Marilyn, Marilyn turned wife; Marilyn sad, happy, high, low, alive, dead. Guiles's book showed me that the Norma Jeans, Rosas, Christines, all of us, are in the life-thing together. The more I see Norma-Jean-Marilyn-the-person, the more I understand that her life was, in some crucial ways, like the rest of ours—she was in some way, *all* women.

Two things seem central to her life and death: (1) the victimization of her by other people and (2) the bottomless pit of her loneliness. I don't know what she actually experienced, but these are my responses to reading about her. And aren't these two experiences common to most all of us?

First, her victimization. A lot of people have seen Marilyn from a psychological point of view as the natural victim because of an unsettled, insecure childhood. Guiles refutes this (although he then embarks on an exposé of the many people who exploited her). He claims that Marilyn herself never "felt completely at home with Marilyn"[1]—a statement I'll come back to later.

Anyway, Christine, I believe she became a moral scapegoat. For example, to Mom and her friends she was the "other" woman. She seduced men openly when Mom and her friends couldn't; she threw off her bathing suit for the photographers when Mom and her friends wouldn't—nor were any photographers waiting if they did! She used her body to become filthy rich, and they wouldn't, not these ladies exalted in the Book of Ruth or the Proverbs. My father and brother looked on, secure they would never leave their wives for such a woman (but of course no such woman appeared!). Marilyn did become rich; she did lose clothes and locks of hair to admirers; she was idolized throughout the world. Until . . .

Her loneliness. She died alone and lonely. Maybe her loneliness is suddenly so important to me today because I'm feeling so lonely. Yet my loneliness is very different from MM's loneliness, as Guiles describes it. It's a difference based on our sense of whom we percieve ourselves to be. That is, I have some sense of an identity that belongs to me, Rosa, and I know at least some of the powers and foibles of that identity called Rosa. But Norma Jean seemed to have little sense of her own powers as Norma Jean. Did she exist as either Norma Jean or Marilyn? She was always looking to producers, husbands, friends, makeup artists, and her audience for confirmation. She needed to be told *who she was.*

I think this looking to others for a sense of identity is experienced by a lot of women, don't you? I mean modern women, you and me, Christine! Ideally we should look like a *Playboy* foldout, write like Edith Sitwell, think like Madam Curie; we ought never to age, never complain, always wear the right clothes, avoid ring-around-the-collar, play a wicked game of golf, be on time, make our gardens grow and our nests flourish. How do we know? We just watch the television screen, consult the department store windows, call the library, attend the class/lecture/seminar, run to the doctor, subscribe to the magazine, tune into the appraising (or disapproving) glances of other women, and of course, *most* especially men! Result? A self-perpetuating anxiety that maybe we are not complete.

My question then is whether Marilyn had more of this anxiety than most of us. In becoming part of the image she had to live with did she lose sight of Norma Jean? And was it loneliness that became the unbearable burden? Maybe the famous Marilyn Monroe had something in common with all of us, all of us who are victims of society's expectations and have little or no real sense of our own identity. For her, the "good life" seemed to be solely the approval of others. They held the power of defining her sense of worth.

Writing this I'm aware of how grateful I am for *your* friendship. We all need other people to help us define our sense of worth, and you are among the people who have most helped me. One secret of survival is never to feel completely overwhelmed by loneliness. A corollary is the knowledge that there is always someone to turn to. I feel that with you and hope you do with me.

May you enjoy your seminar in sunny St. Thomas! I don't know when this letter will catch up with you, but I can close with a bit more enthusiasm than I started. Writing to you has been so good for my spirits today! So I'll try again: HAPPY NEW YEAR!!!

And Adieu,
Rosa

Dear Rosa,

I am sitting on the porch of a little Dutch guest house, Miller's Manor, following my breakfast of fresh pineapple and scrambled eggs and wonderfully pungent coffee. The sea in the distance is that mystical opaque blue of the Aegean (Sophocles heard its long-withdrawing roar long ago) and in the harbor is one of the multitudinous cruise ships that bring Bermuda-shorted travelers ashore to pick up the local rum at bargain prices and cruise the sad tourist shops down by the harbor.

The sun and the sea have not lessened my depression. And now I have your Happy New Year letter which fairly reeks of *your* depression! Your description of yourself alone in the cold dormitory recalls all too vividly to my mind Alvarez's description of Sylvia Plath in her little walk up apartment in London, alone on Christmas Eve just before her suicide.[2] And your dream of the angels of death coming and the apparition of Sarah was terrifying even to me here, far away!

I want to say to you, "Stop! Such non-sense!" But I am not saying that. If it is there, it's there—what Anne Sexton called "the rat inside me, / the gnawing pestilential rat."

That is the rat that eats away all that is of beauty and comfort and meaning in the world and leaves us raw and bleeding. It's the rat that scratches away through the winters of our discontents and the fruits of our summers and keeps us forever in terrible isolation and darkness.

I know that rat well; it started gnawing at me after Michael died. And kept on gnawing away until there was no light anywhere. I felt myself sinking deeper into darkness, slipping down and down, until one night just before Christmas . . .

I remember the pain. It was soul pain. My soul was howling in pain and there was no one to hear it but the gnawing rat. I knew that to end the pain I had to escape, *somehow.*

So many others had done it, and I desired it. I could feel it, taste it, smell it—wet and dank and awe-full. Nothingness. It was Nothingness I wanted. Oh the comfort of it! It said, "Come to me and I will give you rest!" I was slipping into the cistern, and there was no will in me to resist. But then something happened, Rosa. In the black well of darkness beckoning beneath me were giant arms and I knew they were the Everlasting Arms—and they would not let me fall through into the Void. So I lay there in them and cried and cried and cried. Finally all cried out, I started climbing back up into the daylight, bloodying my fingers along the way, clutching and then falling again; at last coming up and out from the slimy, dank sides of the cistern.

Did Marilyn feel herself slipping, too? And were there for her no Everlasting Arms to embrace her? She'd been hoarding the pills for weeks. Getting different prescriptions from different doctors. Then she said goodnight one night to her housekeeper and went into her room and swallowed all the pills. They found her with the phone in her hand.

When I was in my moment of desperation, I used the phone too. I called the only friend who was truly a soul-mate, and I know that her voice, which kept on talking to me on and on and on was the voice of those Everlasting Arms.

I believe during such times the only way we really know we have a soul is if we have a soul-mate to whom we can call. For our own souls are in such pain, it's impossible for them to still hear their own heartbeats. The call to live, at such times, must almost always come from the recognition of self through the voice of the soul-mate. A real mating cry in the truest sense of the word—a cry for life to be regenerated!

My soul-mate talked and talked. Afterwards I slept for a full day and part of another night. The next day I went Christmas shopping. But the gnawing pestilential rat returned. I crossed the street and was hit by a car and knocked down. I was only bruised. But had I stepped off the curb a moment sooner, I would have been killed. The rat laughed. Somehow, I got home and sat huddled in the kitchen, shaking and cold and crying. (The doorbell and the phone rang, but I couldn't move to answer them.) The tears ran in rivers for three days and nights. Then they stopped. I remember reading somewhere that in animals tears function as a disease-prevention, disease-fighting mechanism. But that it's only with the human species that tears are directly connected with emotion, sorrow *and* joy. So after my long, long cry I picked myself up and made myself some toast and tea, and called my friend. The Arms had won again.

I believe I have a strong sense of being, Rosa. But I also know I needed the affirmation of my friend who *knew* that being and who loved it *as it was.*

Existential? Hardly! What I'm saying is that I did not experience my will-to-continue-to-be in totally autonomous terms. I needed the Voice of Another to call me back.

Now what if that other had not been there? Would I still have crawled up into the light just because my time had not yet come? All I know is that the Voice *was* there and that it *did* call me back. I guess that for Marilyn there was no one at the other end of the line. (You may be too young to remember the old hymn "The Royal Telephone," about calling up to Heaven and finding Someone there? Anyway, that's what I felt I did—only my Voice of God was spoken through the voice of my friend who in all humility I believe was given to me *by* God.)

Norma Jean and Marilyn. Did MM exist as either? Or was she truly separated from herself? And to what extent is separation-from-self a necessary corollary to separation-from-others, at least a significant other?

We *are* all related. We can choose to accept or to deny that relatedness, but it remains. One's parents or one's heritage or one's siblings or one's children—they can be rejected, yet the fact of the connectedness remains. We can choose never to go home again, treat our parents like strangers; but then we live in es-strange-ment.

Living as strangers, one to another, one to God. "Which of us has known his [her] maker?" Or "which of us has known his [her] neighbor?"

I came into the knowing of myself through the knowing of this very special friend who recognized my inner self. I think I brought the same self-recognition to her. Thus our friendship was a re-cognition or a re-knowing of our inner selves. Marilyn, on the other hand, received from the outer world no affirmation of her *inner* self but only of a cosmeticized, romanticized version of her *exterior* self. (And there was no one to affirm her *soul.* Only her *body.*)

The little I know of Marilyn's last days is this: She had made *The Misfits,* one of her first pieces of serious acting. Good reviews, but little money. Then her divorce from Arthur Miller, and the death of the man who was her co-star and her fantasy father figure, Clark Gable. Then her studio put her back playing the dumb, sexy blonde role that had kept those dollars coming in. She didn't want to be the dumb, sexy blonde anymore. But there was no one around to affirm her inner self and keep her from saying yes to yet another dumb, sexy blonde type picture.

Like Hemingway she couldn't change scripts, so she

made her exit. It was perhaps the only way she knew to say no once and for all to being the dumb, sexy blonde. What is so sad is that it was her no that was heard by the public and not the yes it implied—the yes to the Marilyn Monroe who wanted to continue her study with the Strassbergs and become a serious actress.

Was her suicide a victory cry over her oppressors? I think so. She was oppressed and kept in her place by a society that knew what they wanted from her and how to get it. (Never mind what *she* wanted!) After her death, one of her producers said of her, "Marilyn Monroe was a phenomenon of nature, like Niagara Falls and the Grand Canyon. You can't talk to it. It can't talk to you. All you can do is stand back and be awed by it."

As a phenomenon of nature, a state of nonbeing was forced upon her. The wonder is not that she finally took upon herself the form of innate matter by killing herself, but that she was able to hold out as long as she did for the *Dasein* way of being ("being-*for*-itself"). I believe her studying with the Strassbergs in New York was partly responsible, as well as her finding family and Catholic roots with Joe Di Maggio, and later family and Jewish roots with Arthur Miller.

Some people have said that she should have stayed with Joe DiMaggio. But I understand he wanted her to stay home and be a housewife and refused to escort her to all the Hollywood parties essential to her career. She had to go alone.

To go alone. How strong one has to be! And if one is a woman, the stronger one becomes the less likely one is to find a mate (who must according to our society be the stronger one).

I am thinking now of how deserted I felt by Michael when he died (killed himself?). We had argued that night over whether or not to do a seminar together. Some friends had invited us to do a seminar on Religion and Literature at a small college near here. Michael felt insulted that he should be put on an equal par with me professionally (his was the reputation after all). I felt hurt, and said that my own perspective as a woman was important and valid and a needed complement to his perceptions. He said he was "sick and tired of hearing about all this women's lib stuff all the time" and stormed out of the house.

Six hours later the phone call came from the state police. His car had skidded off the road in the rain on the highway going out towards Lexington, where his former wife, Zan, lived.

Much of my depression in the months that followed was based on the feeling that he had rejected me, and much of my sense of impotence in my work was due to the fact that I felt he had rejected me because of my professional strength. I had somehow failed him as a woman and had become too manly, and thus had sent him off in the night back to the woman who had "been like a mother to him"— a phrase he himself had often used as a sign of the dis-ease of their relationship. (There was of course some comfort in it too, which *ours* did not have.) Wasn't he strong enough to accept my strength? Or should *I* have made myself weaker to match his weakness? It's so confusing, Rosa.

Arthur Miller may have guessed at some of the frustration Marilyn felt in finding a true soul-mate. But all *he* could do was write about it. So he gave her these lines in *The Misfits:* "If I have to be alone, I'd rather be alone by myself than with someone else."

In her last interview (*Life* magazine, 3 August 1962) she told Richard Meryman, "It might be kind of a relief to be finished. It's sort of like you don't know what kind of a yard dash you're running, but then you're at the finish line and you sort of sigh—you've made it! But you never have—

you have to start all over again." Imagine what it must have been like to have her hair stylist with her wherever she was sent; to have to have a cosmetician and a wardrobe attendant always in the wings; to feel that what she *really was* genuinely and nonartificially was not good enough; to always have to be prepared with the expensive mask that her public paid to see. How *could* she have maintained any sense of her own inner being when she was continually being bought and sold on the looks of her flesh?

It is interesting that both the Soviets and the Vatican understood her and were in agreement about the nature of her fate. At the time of her death *Izvestia* portrayed "Miss Monroe" as an actress whose artistic aspirations had been "stifled and made fun of." It called her death "something bigger than personal tragedy. . . . It has acquired a social significance and pronounced a sentence . . . on a monster which makes a travesty of art, virtue, truth, and nature. . . . The name of this monster is Hollywood."

And the Vatican City newspaper, *L'Osservatore Romano,* called Marilyn a "victim of a symbolic form of life that had been forced on her by other people . . . the victim of a mentality, of a custom, of a concept of life which makes one a symbol."

Our own nation's press concurred. Bosley Crowther wrote in the *New York Times,* "The Monroe personality . . . seemed headed for stronger creations than her early comedies. It was thought by perceptive critics that she might shuck the Monroe symbol in time.

"But . . . she was fashioned into the female image of . . . a 'dumb blonde' of the sort that gentlemen prefer, she was . . . contained within this role. . . . She was made to become a part of the image, and as the image grew into a symbol, a standardization, there was no telling how much she had allowed herself and her own life to be merged and absorbed in it."[3]

And an editorial of the same day declared even more explicitly:

> In a singular sense, the tragic death of film star Marilyn Monroe . . . must be viewed as the dismal culmination of an American tragedy. Miss Monroe was conspicuously the victim of her sad inability to adjust her sensitive nature and tangled ambitions to the peculiarly demanding and synthetic environment in which she lived and worked. . . . Hollywood was selling her body, as it were. It wasn't selling her soul. . . .
>
> The sad and ironic realization is that Miss Monroe sincerely aspired to creativity and quality in the films and perhaps in the theatre. But the effort to overcome the many obstacles to professional expression that were in her way were apparently too great for her.[4]

You might wonder why I have all this information! You know I have been doing some research on women writers and suicide and the occurrence in the work of so many women authors of attempted suicide as a sort of symbolic rebirth experience. Well my interest in women writers has extended to women in the arts. Hence all this data.

Incidentally, the Monroe suicide made the front page of the *New York Times*. (Most suicides don't, as we both know.) In a straight news story, she was called "the contemporary Venus." Again an object of worship, a nonhuman. How can an individual live when he or she is constantly told, "You are not an individual—you are our goddess (or god)"?

The following week an article by Gay Talese in the *New York Times* suggested that Marilyn's suicide might have actually triggered a record number of New York City suicides (twelve) committed the Sunday after her death. The president of the National Save-a-Life League apparently concurred; he recalled that there had been a wave of suicides two decades earlier after the actress Carole Landis had killed herself.

"Many individuals identify with a movie queen or king," according to a New York psychologist quoted by this article, "and the death of one disturbs a little bit of every one of us."

This article also stated that "others speculated that perhaps Sunday's suicides were influenced by the weather. It was sunny, in the eighties; it had been cloudy on Saturday, and rained most of the week. According to a popular theory, suicides are more common on sunny days because the depressed person is more aware then of the contrast between his own condition and that of apparent brightness in the world he sees."[5]

I write to you, Rosa, from sunny St. Thomas. And I hope that until I return to Cambridge and am in contact with you the sun does not shine too brightly this winter in Berkeley!

Fond wishes to you,
Christine

REFLECTIONS

IN THESE letters Christine and Rosa are both using the suicide death of a woman cult heroine of their day to explore their own experiences and thoughts of suicide. Since Christine is in her thirties her identification with the famous film star who died at the age of thirty-six is all the more poignant.

The occasion of the new year brings Rosa a death dream, a dream that reminds her of the end of a love affair, and a time when she came terrifyingly close to committing suicide. Christine responds by relating a similar time in her own life when her husband's death made her feel close to dying, even willing herself dead.

Such reactions are not uncommon preconditions to suicide. The statement by Dr. Joseph Richman (a psychologist with Albert Einstein College of Medicine in New York City) that suicide "is mostly a problem of dealing with love,"[6] comes as no surprise to most of us. Dr. Richman believes that the suicidee kills him or herself instead of the loved one by whom he or she has been hurt. And he notes, "There is an element of sacrifice in this."

Of even greater interest is Dr. Richman's finding that within a family "the suicidal member was usually the 'bad self' for the family, accepting guilt for everyone."[7] Rosa remembers how Marilyn had represented for her "the other woman," the embodiment of sex and sensuality which good girls were not to incorporate within themselves and by which otherwise good men were seduced.

Thus we may see Marilyn Monroe as one whose life and death were indeed sacrifices to the love-starved and/or sex-satiated society which created her. She tried to give to so many what so many thought they needed and desired. If the men of her day needed a sex goddess to satisfy their fantasies so that they could live their day-to-day lives, then Marilyn offered herself to them in this guise at the sacrifice of her own reality, of her own humanity. If the women of her day needed a beautiful, sensuous, sexual evil woman against whom they could measure their own virtues, then Marilyn offered herself to them also, again at the cost of her own essential humanness. (If the cause of self-sacrifice is less than noble, does that necessarily dishonor the sacrifice itself? Or make it any less a sacrifice?) Her continued existence was both a temptation and a threat, and her response was to do away with both. Such an action is not uncommon. The late psychologist Sidney Jourard has suggested that often people destroy themselves in response to invitations from others that they stop living.[8] Are such deaths not to be seen as sacrifices? Suicides committed, perhaps, so that murder is not necessitated?

Jourard's theory gives substantial weight to the argument made by Edwin Schneidman that our existing fourfold classification of deaths—into homicide, accident, natural, and suicide—is oversimplified and inaccurate.[9] Schneidman argues that the old fourfold classification of means of death is "too confusing, primarily because the psychological factors —the individual's intentions, his motivations, and his role in his own demise— are omitted." Schneidman suggests that what is needed is "a classification of death phenomena focused on the individual's *role* in his own demise."

So Christine can wonder if her husband's death in an automobile accident following a heated argument could not well have been more suicidal than accidental. This leads her to an examination of her own role, a blaming of herself, a questioning of her own motivations which plunged her into a despair so deep that only the concerned voice of a living friend convinced her to go on living.

The problem here concerns woman's traditional roles in society. Rosa remembers when there were two kinds of women—the homemaker and the home-breaker. Christine notes her husband's anger at the women's liberation movement, and at her own professional success which seemed to threaten his. Christine asks almost plaintively, "Should I have . . . made myself weaker, to match his weakness?"

Perhaps that is a cry of many women today who like Sarah find themselves still caught between two worlds—one dying, the other waiting to be born. Most women still fail to ever discover their identities because they are playing the conventional role of the "little woman to the big man" or "the woman behind the man." If, as Dr. Matina Horner has suggested, women still make the choice not-to-succeed,[10] isn't this self-abnegation in itself a form of suicide?

Christine was faced with the choice of professional suicide-by-failure or the death of her personal relationship. (Of course, the opposite is often true for men whose professional success is likely to enhance their personal relationships.)

At a meeting of the American Association of Suicidology in Detroit (1972) it was noted that suicides among young women rose rapidly from 1960 to 1970, quite possibly due to the increasing conflict within our society as to what woman's place should be. In one major city alone the suicide rate for women under twenty doubled during those ten years; the rate for women from twenty to twenty-nine nearly quadrupled. Is this a generation of sacrificial ewes? Women who are sacrificing their lives in order not to destroy their men? Or women who are dying as victims in a war for dignity, maturity, and response-ability, the outcome of which is still uncertain?

Clearly to Rosa and Christine Marilyn Monroe has become a symbol of a woman victimized by a society still in its adolescence, a society which willed her to be a plaything (the ideal Playmate) for men's pleasure. When she could no longer play that role, she killed herself.

In the film version of the rock musical *Tommy*, Marilyn is re-created in the form of an enormous plaster statue (a replica of her famous *Seven Year Itch* publicity photo); she is worshiped by fanatical celebrants as though she were the Madonna. "St. Marilyn" is believed capable of performing miraculous cures, all sexual.

Symbolically then, posthumously, Marilyn Monroe may be seen as a martyr to a secular culture seeking salvation not through grace but through sex, not through love but through "an easy lay," not through God but through the genitals, the mammary glands, and the limbs of any sweet sex angel offering relief from pain, in the words of Norman Mailer, a "sweet heaven-haven of sex."

Rosa and Christine are here writing to one another as women for whom Marilyn is almost a sister. As Rosa says, most women know the anxiety of trying to please men. So many ads and commercials enforce these fears and uncertainties about physical attractiveness. None urge women to cultivate their inner selves. Few even suggest that any such inner self exists because this inner self cannot be packaged or marketed.

Rosa and Christine are both concerned with their inner selves, and to them Marilyn Monroe's suicide means an acknowledgement of the importance of a soul-mate (not a Playmate), who can call out the life-from-within, especially in moments of crisis.

Earlier we spoke of ethicist John Bennett's insistence that the Church should be "the voice for those who have no voice." Certainly this should be true regarding women's place in society. Yet often heard today are the words of the biblical Paul, writing almost 2000 years ago, commanding women to "keep silence in the church."

In opposition to this, a latter-day Paul, theologian Paul Tillich, has written of the need for "the courage to be," in both women and men. This courage to be is rooted in the belief that we are all a part of Being Itself (or, what Tillich calls, "the God above the God of theism"). This concept calls for a transcendence of our anthropomorphic concept of a male God (one that Tillich would call idolatrous) so that woman can be free to identify directly with Being Itself.

The Church has failed to take this task of liberation upon itself, even though the most conservative as well as the most liberal of its spokesmen proclaim that everyone *knows* that God is NOT A MAN. Yet the heresy of a male God continues by the continued use of the exclusively male pronoun for God. Thus woman per se is still excluded from anything but a secondary place in the *king*dom and so feels she "is not" unless she "is" in relation to and through a man. It has only been recently in the writings of such brilliant women theologians as Anne McGraw Bennett, Nelle Morton, Mary Daly, Rosemary Radford Reuther, and Letty Russell, that "Woman's Voice" has even begun to be heard in the churches!

Surely the lack of the courage to be without a man (or many men) was an element in Marilyn Monroe's suicide. In a letter she wrote shortly before her death to her former husband Joe DiMaggio—a letter which was found unmailed in her desk—she spoke of her desire to make *him completely happy* and said, if only she could do that, she would have succeeded in "the most important task of my life."[11]

But somewhere Marilyn knew that the answer was more complex. Her last interview quoted in Christine's letter shows she was questioning the whole prison of her

Hollywood life. Søren Kierkegaard, tormented Danish Christian philosopher of the century before, said that the two basic questions were always these: "How did I get into this and how do I get out of it again; how does it end?" As Marilyn said to *Life* interviewer, Richard Meryman, "It might be kind of a relief to be finished." And as Guiles notes, she "had been taken seriously by too few, too late" and "her place in American life, her value, was made clear only after she was gone.[12]

What may we learn from Marilyn Monroe's suicide? What might it teach us about our own lives, our own values, and about our society? Is it possible that Marilyn died so that other women might live with more "courage to be" from within—with less dependence on the approval of a thoroughly externally secularized and sexualized society? Is it possible that Marilyn might have been a martyr, in her own way, to the cause of liberation of the spirit of all women and of all men? Her death, an affirmation that true nobility may sell its flesh but not its soul?

Many new liberation theologians such as Guiterrez, Segundo, Daly, and Morton express one interpretation of the message of Christ to mean the message of liberation. To die for Christ would mean, then, to die for the cause of liberation. In retrospect, we may say that Marilyn Monroe's self-imposed death set her and perhaps others, free at last.

"Let him who is without sin among you cast the first stone." These were Jesus' words to the Pharisees who had brought the adulterous woman to him to be stoned (John 8:1–11). He insisted, instead, that they all own up to their own adulterous motives through which the woman had been victimized.

Perhaps if our society had acknowledged its part in the victimization of Marilyn Monroe earlier, she would not have had to choose the path of suicide as a way to own her own freedom.

CHAPTER 5

LINDA MARIE DUNNE:
To Such Belongs the Kingdom

2 February
Berkeley

Dear Christine,

Your letter arrived in the morning mail. I brought it up to my room, made a cup of Red Zinger tea, and snuggled beneath my patchwork comforter to read it. That was over an hour ago, and I should be preparing for tomorrow's anatomy exam but I must write to you first.

I can't get over us—our lives—our letters. I simply can't get over the fact that we've known each other for eight years and still know so little about each other. All these years of knowing each other and writing to each other, and we've only just shared the life/death secret! Corresponding for months about the suicides of Sarah, Charlotte Perkins Gilman, Hemingway and Marilyn Monroe, and only just now telling each other that we *almost* did the deed ourselves!

All this time discussing other's suicide depressions as if they had nothing to do with us! I remember years ago the Boston psychiatrist Avery Weisman saying that everyone is potentially suicidal. At that time I didn't believe him. But since my own experience with Paul (and now reading your letter) I'm beginning to believe he's right. I must say, I just couldn't believe that such things were going on inside *you.* You're such a *strong* person that it never occurred to me when I wrote to you about *my* depression that you might be needing *my* caring and support as much as I was needing yours! Christine, your letter reminded me again that we die so many times before the final dying. Who said, "There are so many little dyings that it doesn't matter which one of them is death"? We do die, I mean *really* die when we lose somebody we love.

I remember sitting by a woman's bedside asking her about herself, the feelings she had when the doctor told her she had cancer and was going to die. She said, "Well, I cried for two days straight. Then I decided to get busy and live the rest of my life instead of just letting it seep away."

"Two days? You only cried for two days?" I asked. Then I told her about crying for two days over my disappointment when I was turned down at the last minute for a hospital job I wanted desperately, she reached out and took my hand. My hand seemed so strong and big in her wrinkled, trembling one. She squeezed it, looked me straight in the eye, and said, "But you must understand that when my daughter died, I cried for six years."

It was the first time that anyone had helped me understand how much dying (and grieving) we do along the way. Surely you, Christine, *did* die in a way after Michael's death and were reborn.

I'm thinking of you now with special caring. In fact, I'll light a candle here in my room as a symbol of the "flame" of life that keeps us going during the rough times. (That way when you feel your flame flickering you can look west for some extra energy!)

As for me, I think the worst of my slump is over. *Finally* the second semester got under way. The others returned to the dorm. Also, I decided to get away the second weekend in January. I drove down the coast. It started out as a wandering, goalless trip. I spent the first night outside of Monterey and the next morning I decided to return to a little Scottish bakery in Pacific Grove where Paul and I had once had tea. I ordered scones and tea and sat at the same table where we had sat. That started a sort of reclaiming journey. I headed south to many of the places he and I had shared—Nepenthe, Big Sur . . . For some crazy reason it was really healing to do that. I thought I would never be able to go back there without him, but found to my surprise that the beauty was still there, just as it was when we had been together.

On the last night I found the spot beside the ocean where we had sat on the rocks, listening to the waves beat against the shore and watching the hypnotic spin of a lighthouse beam revolving in the distance. I stayed several hours, shivering in the dampness, but feeling very much at one with the sea and stars. Sometime in the early morning I got back in my car and drove all the way home. When I got to my room I made a cup of hot tea, but before I finished it I had fallen into a deep, sweet sleep that lasted for over twelve hours. When I woke up I felt like a butterfly emerging from her cocoon. Almost—perhaps not quite—ready to fly.

Well it's a good thing! The following Friday night I had an unexpected visitor—*Geoff!!*

As you know, Geoff and I were only acquaintances when Sarah was alive. In fact, I didn't really like him and thought he was all wrong for her—as mismated in their way as Paul and I had been in ours. So we just stood there looking at each other. Finally his face became all contorted and he started to stammer, and we were at last able to embrace each other.

He said he wanted to talk with me because he had heard from some students that I had been counseling people following Sarah's death. I told him it was hardly counseling —that I had as many questions and as much grief about her dying as anyone else.

Anyway we went up to my room to talk. (I do wish there was a comfortable, private place to talk except our own closet-y rooms!!). He began by saying he was out here spending the holidays with his brother, whose wife had just had a baby, and that he needed to talk to someone who would understand his feelings. Then he slumped down into the same chair Sarah had been sitting in during our last fateful talk. He put his head in his hands and choked out the words, "If Sarah hadn't done that, you know, I'd be a father any day now."

Well I was speechless. My first reaction was to hit, kick, do anything to hurt him, my mind crazy with Sarah's last conversation. Geoff had *abandoned* her in her pregnancy and literally *driven* her to have an abortion. Didn't he know there would NOT have been a baby? But now this self-assured young man was sobbing and my anger dissolved in sadness. Once again, nothing made sense to me about Sarah's death. We sat there in silence.

Finally we began to talk a little. I told him all the facts I knew about Sarah's death. Small comfort. He told me that he had felt so ambivalent about the whole situation (of marrying her, her being pregnant) that he'd really misread Sarah's responses (you know how glib she'd act about the things that touched her the most deeply—her old survival technique that really failed in the end). He said that she kept telling him she wasn't sure she wanted to be married now, and that he should go on to Atlanta for a year so they could have more time to decide. He stuck to that version of the story in spite of my telling him that she said *he* was the one who really didn't want the marriage right away. He also said that when she mentioned abortion he had said it was up to her, and that he would pay for it if she chose to do that, but admitted that the whole scene around that conversation was pretty fuzzy now—and the implications of it were terrifying to him. He told me then that he's been seeing a psychiatrist for four months. He feels he's worked through the worst of his guilt, but he's still walking around with her memory deep inside his belly like a corpse.

Christine, I was at a loss as to what to say: I told him how little we know about suicide—who does it, and who doesn't, whether motives are important, and whether other people are important and can be considered responsible.

Geoff said he could understand an old, senile person with some terminal disease not wanting to go on any longer. But Sarah was young and healthy. So I told him about the suicide of a young girl which has haunted me ever since it happened some years ago.

Linda Marie Dunne.

Don't look for her in history books or movie magazines or even in a psych book. She's in some faded newspaper columns, now microfilmed and stashed away for researchers like me. Linda Marie Dunne was a young woman, age twenty-one, living with her parents in Arco, Nevada. She was going steady with an Air Force lieutenant stationed there—and I assume her parents didn't like him or thought she should marry somebody from her own home town. Anyway, one Friday night she stayed out all night. Her parents decided that Linda needed a lesson. They would teach her about giving up love. They would force her to surrender Beauty, the collie that had been her close companion since she was ten. Her Dad and Mom drove

Linda and Beauty out into the desert where they ordered her to dig a deep hole. She must have been confused and terrified, but she obeyed them. Then her father ordered her to shoot Beauty and handed her a 22-caliber pistol. Linda's mother was holding Beauty on a short leather leash. Linda hesitated for a moment; her father again ordered her, "Shoot!" She put the pistol to her right temple and shot herself.

At the first reporting of the story, the police said the only charge that could be filed against the parents was cruelty to animals. Later the charge of involuntary manslaughter was brought against them on the basis that they knew their daughter's emotional state when they gave her the loaded pistol. But the coroner's jury had already returned a verdict of suicide.[1]

This case has haunted me. Imagine the horror her parents must have felt. Her father was reported to have called out, "I killed her! I killed her! It's just like I killed her myself!" And did he? How free was Linda? Was the choice really between Beauty and herself? What unresolved guilt must have been operating in this twenty-one-year-old girl-woman to have had her capitulate to such treatment? And what sort of sin did her father and mother believe she had committed to make them enforce such a punishment upon their child-become-a-woman?

I tried to get the idea across to Geoff that we often don't know what motivates a person to commit suicide. Why did Linda choose to kill herself rather than her dog or her parents? Why did Sarah choose suicide rather than one of the other alternatives? Then he said, "How old was Linda Marie Dunne?" And I told him again. "She was twenty-one," a little younger than Sarah. She was at the age of "independence." But what does that mean? I'm twenty-nine. I'm twenty-nine and still don't consider myself "grown-up" or truly "independent"! What or when is "the age of responsibility"? Certainly it has nothing to do with the arbitrary limits the law sets upon it!

Anyway, after all of this talk, it was about 2:00 A.M. and I was exhausted and ready for bed. But Geoff began crying again and wanting to return again and again for every detail about Sarah.

He kept on sobbing about "becoming a father any day now" if "Sarah hadn't done that." I was at my wit's end. I made some more tea, which kept me busy. Can you imagine Sarah and the baby living? And Geoff acknowledging his role as father? I found it impossible and still do. Anyway, more about his story.

He'd just come from the funeral of his cousin, a fourteen-year-old boy named Donald. Donald had contracted polio when he was six and been confined to a wheelchair ever since. He'd seemed like a cheerful kid, had become very involved in his church youth group, had had friends, and had done well in school. Then three nights ago his parents found him in the bathtub with a bullet in his head. He'd left a note which Geoff had with him: "Please give my money in my bank to the March of Dimes. Have the people who come to the funeral give the money to the March of Dimes instead of flowers. Again, I am sorry to do this. With love, Donald."

Geoff was wondering if out of my experience working with disabled children I could offer any insights into why Donald took his life. I asked about the family and whether anybody had noticed some new despair about the boy's physical disability. Nobody had. Donald had seemingly adjusted to his wheelchair existence in spite of the obvious limitations on his boyhood activity. (That doesn't surprise me much, because most of the kids I've worked with have shown amazing resiliency when faced with what we adults see as overwhelming obstacles.) However, I pointed out to

Geoff that a child certainly would be capable of feeling that he was not worthwhile—not fully human—because of being confined to a wheelchair. But I would doubt whether someone like Donald would see his disability as an end to usefulness the way Charlotte Perkins Gilman viewed hers. My experience with kids has taught me that they don't often think of themselves as being useless, or being a burden. They do have fantasies of being *more useful* by disappearing (possibly they may often hear from their families such phrases as "get lost," "be quiet—leave me alone") and, that, like Tom Sawyer, they may succeed in getting a whole community to admit their love for them by disappearing.[2] But they really don't struggle—in the way that we adults do—with the problem of needing to appear autonomous and fully independent. Because kids are so dependent on adults for their physical existence, they are probably more able to accept dependence due to physical limitations caused by disease or accidents. They see vulnerability as a given.

I told Geoff that a fourteen-year-old might also seek some comfort that isn't forthcoming in earthly relationships and long to be received into some other world! Donald might have believed that by ending his physically limited existence he would immediately find wholeness and acceptance as a normal teenage boy.

As you know, the need to be considered physically desirable becomes especially acute during adolescence. Now I'm thinking of the many cases of *anorexia nervosa* which have been appearing in recent years. Of those affected by this bizarre disease, 80 percent are female, mostly in their early teens. They are usually intelligent, middle or upper-class girls who start to diet and then simply stop eating altogether, sometimes losing fifty pounds or so in a few months and continuing on to a point of malnutrition from which there is no return. They literally starve themselves to death. Could they be in some way victims of our cultural expectations of women?[2] (Women should be thin, like fashion models. Similarly, men should be big and strong like football heroes.)

That leads me to ask you, Christine, whether you think most people who kill themselves are really looking for comfort and healing—the Everlasting Arms as you say. Maybe everyone who does it is in a place where they feel totally vulnerable like little kids and believe that their hope for comfort lies beyond this world. If there is any chance that that is the case, isn't it hard to understand how God would pubish them for *that?* Is Donald at fourteen accountable for his actions as a member-in-community? At what point does a person become responsible for his or her own soul, and for actions that affect the welfare of other people? And does that responsibility remain with a person in all circumstances? For instance, is it the same when a person is in great suffering, becomes emotionally disturbed, or is being tortured?

Maybe these questions are contingent on whether God is a loving or punishing God. I grew up thinking of God as a combination Good Humor Ice Cream Man and wrathful school principal. I now know God is neither of these. But sometimes when I'm thinking about death there is a part of me that wonders if there isn't some terrible punishment for suicide.

I know very little of how children nowadays conceive of God, but my studies have revealed that children commit suicide in far greater numbers than anyone realizes, and lately I've been wondering if perhaps it could be that *we are all children in the sight of God.*

I'm off an another digression, but I know it has a point. I remember this film about autistic children (kids who have virtually committed suicide by withdrawing into worlds of their own where no one can communicate with them and vice versa). I watched a woman therapist work with three or four such children individually. Her method was simple. Instead of trying to reach the child with our language, she undertook to learn the child's language, which for most of these children consisted primarily of body movement, often highly ritualized, sometimes seemingly totally random.

This amazingly sensitive therapist followed each child around a room for hours at a time copying the child's body patterns. Then after months of doing this, she would begin occasionally to introduce variations of her own. Eventually the child would begin to follow her *new* motion. Trust had been gained; communication established. Therapist and autistic child had a common union, a common language.

Now if every individual in the world had someone who truly spoke his or her language . . . I can't finish that sentence. What then? I don't know. But it reminds me of an article I read recently that's going to stir up a lot of controversy.[3]

It's written by Sheldon B. Kopp. A distinguished therapist and author of the book, *If You Meet the Buddha on the Road, Kill Him.* The case concerns twenty-year-old Penny. When Penny was finally referred to Dr. Kopp from her regular therapist, a Dr. M., she had already attempted suicide three times and had carved into the skin of her left arm the letter D, the letter E, and the letter A. She explained to Dr. Kopp that when then final letter D was also there, that's what she would be—D E A D.

Penny's regular therapist had been trying a variety of ways to thwart Penny's "final" suicide attempt. Dr. Kopp decided to use another approach.

He asked Penny if she were firmly decided on suicide. She said yes. He pondered this for awhile and then said he was sorry she had made this decision, but since she had made it he would respect it and help her carry it through successfully. Then he asked her for some details about how she was going to do it, and suggested certain changes that would make her attempt more likely to succeed (e.g., discouraging her from taking LSD beforehand; encouraging her to take some sort of sedative instead). At the end of the interview he told her that if for any reason at all she changed her mind, he would really look forward to seeing her at the same time the following week. They shook hands.

The next week Penny appeared on schedule. Dr. Kopp (greatly relieved!) asked her why she had decided not to follow through on her act. He asked if anything he had said had contributed to her decision to remain alive.

Penny's reply was, " 'What you did for me was best. Was to be just where *I was*. Whenever I tell anybody about my craziness, or how unhappy I am, or how I want to kill myself, all they do is criticize. They get scared and they try to change my mind. *You didn't criticize.* If I wanted to kill myself you said you'd help me do it. The way you talked to me, I didn't have to feel guilty. So I didn't feel like killing myself any more. Besides I wanted to come with Dr. M. to see you some more.' "

In short, Christine, what Dr. Kopp had done was to affirm Penny's *self.* He affirmed *her* in the only way he knew how on such short notice—by affirming the one act she most wanted and could act out independent of all the other realities around her. And it was this affirmation which she needed to go on living. He took a gamble—a terrifying gamble—but it worked!

Well, enough disgressions. Geoff and I talked all night. Finally, towards dawn, he proclaimed that he thought Donald and Sarah were similar in the sense that they had both chosen the only path they saw open to them. I asked how he'd come to this conclusion. He shrugged his slim shoulders and said, "Well, they DID it, didn't they?" Then he said, "I guess, we do all have our separate paths to take. Sometimes I wish I could change the one I'm on, but I don't see how I can. Do you see any way of changing the path of your life?" I told him I didn't . . . Christine, that acknowledgement frightened me. But I don't know why.

Finally, we talked about what Donald's parents—or Geoff—could have done for young Donald. It was a strange discussion because I know we were both really trying to figure out what we might have done differently for Sarah. Geoff suddenly recalled Donald *had* once mentioned killing himself. But nobody seemed to listen or take it seriously. I suspect it was just too fearsome for his parents to admit that their child could actually want to kill himself. Could this be why children's deaths are rarely reported as suicide? The parents fear and perhaps suspect that they haven't given their child enough love or money or God-only-knows-what. So they interpret the suicide as an accident. (Donald's death, for instance, was reported as an accident!)

Well, Geoff's back in Atlanta now. I told him to write, and I'm sure he will. Meanwhile dear friend, remember the candle here in Berkeley burns for you there in Cambridge.

Adieu, and many loving thoughts
Rosa

Dear Rosa,

Thank you for lighting the candle for me. Keep it
burning. I'm in bed with the flu and you know what that
does for one's morale. We used to sing a song in Sunday
School— "This little candle light of mine . . ."

I'd forgotten that song, and how much it used to mean
to me till you mentioned keeping the candle burning as a
symbol of keeping my flame alive. Thank you. Every time I
feel like snuffing mine out or letting someone else blow it
out, I'll think of your candle burning for me across the
continent.

I'm glad for your healing drive down the coast to
Nepenthe and Big Sur. Yes, I know how it is to purge the
spirits from those places that you have once shared with a
loved one. It's part of a reclaiming of life—of your own life
which *must go on* though the connection with that other life
has been severed. I had to do that here, up around the coast
near Rockport in Maine where Michael and I had bought
some land the summer before we were married, land to
retire on on an island south of Bar Harbor. I went there last
summer and camped out alone in a pup tent. In the middle
of the night a roebuck appeared, stomped the ground,
snorted, and then retreated. No trace of him by daylight, but
I no longer felt lonely there.

I did have a great feeling of solitude. May Sarton
distinguishes between the two: "Loneliness is the poverty of
self; solitude is the richness of self."[4]

Self. What do I mean when I speak of "my-self" or you,
of "your-self"? The semantic implication seems to be that

there is a part of me, an essential part of me which belongs solely to me, and a corresponding part of you which belongs solely to you. "My-self," says the dictionary, is the *intensive* form of "I." "Myself" is not only the subject "I," acting in the world, but also is the part of me which lies buried *beneath* the "I." "Myself" remains though there may be no "I" acting in the world.

It is the "self" which remains when the "I" vanishes. And it is the "self" which stands in direct relation to God. You mention in your letter that often children may think they can "be more useful by disappearing." It seems to me that it is the "I" they try to make disappear, and that perhaps they have not yet learned to distinguish between the "I" and the "self."

You say that children don't usually think of themselves as burdens, perhaps because they are used to being dependent. But up to what age can that be true? You seem to imply that some change takes place at about Donald's age —about the time of puberty—the time when in most cultures the boy is said to become a man and the girl a woman.

I would agree that at puberty the feeling of dependency no longer seems appropriate to the growing child. It's the time when the age of reason is said to begin—the age of accountability to the community. Our country has put the legal age boundaries at eighteen or twenty-one for men and women; it varies from state to state, though such legal definitions have nothing to do with one's true state of maturity!

I recently read an article the tone of which was clever and satiric. In it, the author argued that suicide should not be considered a social evil. "I am, however, firmly opposed to the free suicide of minors. Death, like Bach, is a complex and sophisticated affair. Even among mature, experienced adults, very few can understand it fully. I do not favor a lowering of the suicide age to eighteen."[5]

Again I take refuge in the individual situation. It may be true that "death, like Bach, is a complex and sophisticated affair." But so is life. And some lives are more complex than others.

The "age of responsibility" has nothing (or little) to do with chronology. Think of the people we have been discussing: Donald (fourteen), Linda Marie Dunne (twenty-one), Sarah (twenty-four), Marilyn Monroe (thirty-six), Hemingway (sixty-two), and Charlotte Perkins Gilman (seventy-five). Ages fourteen to seventy-five; puberty to old age; the autonomous decision to die. What does chronology have to do with the age of responsibility or the age of reason? I believe the age of responsibility begins when an individual becomes aware of his or her place in the whole, the larger community. There must be a sliding scale for this age—it must exist at any given time to greater or lesser degrees. For some it may never exist. On the other hand, as you yourself know so well, there are very young children—nine or ten years old—who seem to be very aware of what's going on in their worlds and who appear to have reached an age of reason and responsibility *not* reached by many adults. And so we return to the mystery.

What of those times when adults feel like little children? For instance, I watched a friend's ninety-year-old grandfather die last summer. In the last weeks of a life that had known love, power, and modest fame, he was reduced to a weak, childlike baby weighing ninety pounds at most. We held hands and he spoke in a whisper. He told me that he had learned a Bible verse as a child which at last he understood: "Suffer the little children to come unto me." I realized then that in his final unrelenting suffering he had both misinterpreted and fully interpreted the word *suffer*. Having lived nearly a century he was able to let go of his autonomy in time to be received. He didn't commit suicide, but he met death straight on through suffering, and I *watched* him surrender at last to the Everlasting Arms.

How different and truly beautiful it would be if all potential suicidees could be sure, truly certain, of the Everlasting Arms waiting to give welcome. If we were absolutely certain they were there, how many more of us would try to get to them for comfort? Could that be why God has placed an element of doubt in our faith—just to keep us going on with this play of life? If it is true, as I remember Reverend Helm in my home Evangelical and Reformed church in Blue Island, Illinois, saying that "God has no hands but ours to do his work on earth," could it be that the Creator has given us doubt enough to keep us going on about our work before going home to seek our Maker? I think those who take their lives in a serious, premeditated, rational manner are those who have come to a certain conclusion: absolute belief or absolute disbelief. That is, either they are certain of the Everlasting Arms waiting to receive them, or certain that there are no Everlasting Arms at all.

I can't conclude this letter without commenting upon your meeting with Geoff! It must have been an excruciating experience for you! It seems as if the listening and responding that you weren't able to do for Sarah, you were able to do for Geoff in Sarah's name.

From all our talk now, I see a principle emerging. It is that total affirmation by a *significant other* dissuades one from suicide. Sarah didn't have that significant other. Nor did any of the other "successful" suicides we've discussed, except possibly Sarah's grandfather.

Statistics show that most successful suicidees *have* threatened and/or attempted suicide previously. But there are no statistics on those cases like Penny's—or yours and mine—of the individuals who talked about it but have *not* done it because someone really listened and stayed present!

Linda Marie Dunne / 109

This brings me back to *us*. As you said, we've been "corresponding for months about other people" while carrying our own heavy burdens. But I think it's also true that at some level we have also been writing about ourselves. We've both been aware that in talking about Sarah (and Charlotte, and Ernest, and Marilyn, and all the others), we've been talking about a significant part of our *selves*, that each of of us needs affirmed.

I need then to ask you about one comment in your last letter which still worries me, Rosa. When Geoff asked you if you thought you could "change the path of your life" you answered "no." Then you found yourself "rather frightened" by that reply. What is this fright about, Rosa? Can you tell me?

Meanwhile, know that a candle burns also on this coast for you, to in-spirit you through these dreary winter months. We've had sleet and ice for two weeks. I hate to go out—even to the class I love to teach! (Wasn't there snow last winter in the Berkeley hills?)

Well, good friend, this is my valentine to you. It comes with love. Let me hear from you soon.

Fondly,
Christine

P.S. Rosa, there is another whole realm of speculation in regard to suicide which we have not yet discussed and about which I know little. A recent incident has stimulated my thinking in this realm:

One of the local churches recently had its annual pre-Lenten retreat for its high school youth group at a retreat center out toward Waltham. I have spoken at this church several times and know many of the congregation. The minister called me last Tuesday. A seventeen-year-old boy had wandered off from the group and was found hours later hanging from a birch tree in the forest.

Jon was a bright young man by any standards—a Merit Scholar and a scientist, also interested in philosophy. But he'd been depressed following a kidney ailment and the day before his suicide his best friend had taken up with the girl he'd had a crush on all year. When my minister friend, Todd, told me about this, I immediately thought of a book I'd just been reading on acupuncture. It claimed that kidney problems may be related to suicide-proneness:

> . . . The basic medium for life is water. The Controller of Water is the kidney energy system. . . . The kidney energy system . . . governs the will of man to survive and evolve. . . .
>
> The kidneys perform their basic work with the aid of the bladder. . . . If these systems become unbalanced, the organism begins to "drown" in its own wastes. . . . Like a drowning person, the individual has no time for others in his life; he is too busy trying to save himself. . . . the constant threat of "going under" looms in the background. Total insecurity of the organism ensues, leading to insanity and sometimes suicide.[6]

I quoted this passage to Todd and he reacted almost violently. He felt such an interpretation was hopelessly reductionistic and mechanistic. Suddenly I did, too! But then I begin to wonder. How much of our depression, how many of our abnormal behaviors are determined by chemical imbalances? And could we all be made perfectly normal (is it perfect to be normal?) by being chemically balanced? And how many of our greatest writers and artists and religious leaders might be said to have been "unbalanced"?) Again, this is a realm I don't know much about. I need your help. Do please answer on the basis of any experience you may have had within the medical field.

REFLECTIONS

IN THIS exchange of letters, Rosa and Christine write of the suicides of young people and raise the question of when the "age of responsibility" begins for one's own life. Christine suggests this age has "nothing (or little) to do with chronologies," but more to do with the ability to respond in a meaningful way to the immediate surrounding community. The age of responsibility, she insists, begins with the individual's awareness of his or her place in the whole. And she notes that there are many adults who may never be said to have come to an age of accountability.

And again, Christine presents us with the question of to whom *does* one's life belong? If a child's life does not irrefutably belong to the child, does it belong to the parents? The question is most poignantly dramatized by Rosa's story of Linda Marie Dunne, the twenty-one-year-old woman who killed herself while being punished by her parents. (This suicide seems to affirm the results of a study done several years ago by two doctors at the Los Angeles County General Hospital. The study focused on fifty adolescent suicide-attempt patients. The result presented to the 1965 annual meeting of the American Public Health Association showed that 74 percent of the adolescent suicide attempters were in a state of extreme conflict with their families. The study also showed that one-fifth of the suicide attempters had had a parent who had attempted suicide; and over one-fifth of the female attempters were either pregnant or believed themselves to be so at the time of the attempt.)

Christine's letter suggests that in the eyes of God we may all be children. She tells the story of the grandfather of her friend who, as he lay dying, repeated the saying of Jesus, "Suffer the little children . . ."

The biblical phrase the old man repeated may be found in Matthew 19:13–15. Jesus is in Judea surrounded by throngs of followers seeking to be healed, and also by the Pharisees who harrass him with questions regarding technicalities of the old Jewish law. At the end of one such testing exchange some small children are brought up to Jesus "that he might lay his hands on them and pray." Jesus' disciples rebuke the parents, but Jesus says, "Suffer the little children to come unto me and forbid them not, for to such belongs the kingdom of heaven." Then he "laid his hands on them" before he went away.

We can imagine Jesus' state of mind at the end of a long day among the ailing multitudes and the Pharisees, intent upon protecting their own place within the Jewish society and therefore dedicated to the destruction of this man who threatened to reduce all the law (their source of livelihood) to two commandments, "Thou shalt love the Lord thy God with all thy heart, and with all thy soul, and with all thy mind, and thy neighbor as thyself."

It is little wonder that in the relatively guileless faces of the little children rather than in the legalistic minds of the Pharisees, Jesus saw heaven.

Now let us superimpose this scene of Jesus in Judea with that described in Rosa's letter of Linda Marie Dunne in the desert outside Arco, Nevada. She had spent the previous Friday night with her boyfriend. (Love.) Her father was intent on punishing her. (Law.) The punishment was to be the killing of her beloved dog, Beauty. (Law over Love.) She responded by killing herself instead of her dog (Love over Law—"Greater love hath no one than this . . .")

Are we to say that her father was more responsible (i.e., response-able) than Linda? Would she have been more responsible had she killed Beauty instead of herself? To what would she have been responding had she obeyed her father's orders? To what was she responding when she refused to obey them? Could it have been some higher law than that which he represented? Could she have been some modern-day Antigone? How are we to judge Linda?

Rosa, in her letter, discusses her childhood concepts of the judging vs. the loving God and remembers the idea of an "unforgivable sin" which was associated in her mind with suicide. This association still holds true for many people.

But the few modern theologians who have written directly about suicide tend not to perpetrate the idea that suicide is "the unforgivable sin." Dietrich Bonhoeffer, for example, writing of the "temptation to suicide" at the end of the section of his *Ethics* dealing with suicide, concludes, "But who would venture to say that God's grace and mercy cannot embrace and sustain even a man's failure to resist this hardest of all temptations?"[7]

Bonhoeffer's fellow German theologian Karl Barth, in his *Church Dogmatics,* was reluctant to accept the concept of a God to whom any sin would be unforgivable. Wrote Barth,

> If there is forgiveness of sins at all . . . there is surely forgiveness for suicide. The opinion that it alone is unforgiveable rests on the false view that the last will and act of man in time, because they are the last and take place as it were on the very threshold of eternity, are authoritatively and conclusively decisive for his eternal destiny and God's verdict on him. But this cannot be said of any isolated will or act of man, and therefore not even of the last. God sees and weighs the whole of human life. He judges the heart. And He judges it according to His own righteousness which is that of mercy. He thus judges the content of the last hour in the context of the

whole. Even a righteous man may be in the wrong at the last. Even the most sincere believer may be hurled on his death-bed into the most profound confusions and uncertainty, even though there be no suggestion of suicide. What would become of him if there were no forgiveness at this point? Yet if there is forgiveness for him, why not for the suicide?

Here as elsewhere, however, God's forgiveness is no excuse, much less justification, for sin.[8]

Neither Bonhoeffer nor Barth accepted the idea of suicide as the unforgivable sin. But Barth differs from Bonhoeffer in that he says, "Suicide cannot be extenuated, excused or justified. Freedom before this God, the only true God, cannot be freedom for suicide." Whereas Bonhoeffer declares, "Without freedom to sacrifice one's life in death, there can be no freedom towards God, there can be no human life."[9]

The question here is not whether or not suicide is ever justified or whether or not suicide is a sin, but whether suicide is the *unforgivable* sin. We agree with Rosa that the answer is predicated upon what one believes to be the nature of God.

The question of the unforgivable sin is really the question of whether or not we believe in a God who would condemn forever and without hope an individual who had performed one given act, regardless of how that individual had lived the rest of his or her life.

CHAPTER 6

QUANG DUC:
Let Your Light So Shine

4 March
Berkeley

Dear Christine,

Whose line is it—"The hounds of spring are on winter's traces?" My memory of it is from a Thurber cartoon, but something tells me it has loftier beginnings.

Beginnings! Today I saw a robin, the first of the season, and the crocuses are poking up through the crusty soil outside the student union building. And I've started jogging! I'm out every morning puffing around the campus in my new Adidas running shoes. It feels great! My body gets into the rhythm of running and allows my mind to sail freely!

You asked why I was frightened at the thought of not being able to "change my script." Good question. I guess what I'm really afraid of, Christine, is being so *human*—so *mortal!* Perhaps my awareness of this has been heightened through our correspondence. I want to believe that I have almost limitless possibilities just waiting for me to beckon them, even if I never *will* beckon them. But there are times when I know that isn't true.

Let me first respond to your question about the relationship between body chemical imbalances and certain mental states. Well, there's a lot of research being done, mostly in regard to the condition called "schizophrenia." And a lot of suffering is being alleviated through drugs. But I have serious reservations about defining an abnormality solely in terms of body chemistry imbalances. Such explanations discount the need for any further explanations. Is a vision *only* a biochemically induced hallucination? Is an act of martyrdom *only* the result of an irregularity in a person's endocrine system? Such explanations are too simple. They restrict the definition of many phenomena to one realm: the scientific (a realm limited by its own methodology). But there are other spheres of reality, for instance, the religious.

A good person to illustrate the inadequacy of defining suicide only in terms of chemical imbalance came up in a discussion recently . . .

I talked to a young Buddhist monk who had known Quang Duc from the time the young monk was just a little child. When Quang Duc poured gasoline over himself in 1963, igniting it to draw attention to the plight of the eight million Buddhists in Vietnam, this man was only thirteen years old. But he saw the incident and he says, "The image of Quang Duc has seared itself into my heart forever." For him, Quang Duc has become both a symbol and a source of inspiration.

Christine, how are we to explain all those self-immolations by Buddhist monks and nuns? Given positive medical proof that they all had been in a state of chemical imbalance, I would still think, "But is that the whole story??"

What about the larger world and cosmic contexts in which we all live and move? Do you remember, for instance, Jan Palach, who set fire to himself in 1969, hoping his suicide would prevent the Soviet invasion of Czechoslovakia? And the many Americas who killed themselves to protest our involvement in Vietnam?

Were all of these people deranged, as the newspapers often portrayed them? Or chemically imbalanced? Or were they responding to some reality that exceeds our own limited vision and science's measurement tools? Were their deaths a shameful waste or a powerful witness?

My young Buddhist friend believes all the suicides I mentioned are related, and that they all share the element of *witness*. None of them can be thought of as isolated individual deaths. Rather, these people are bound by a common cause, *giving witness*. They have ceased to exist as isolated human beings: they have *become* their cause. These Vietnamese sympathizers and Buddhist monks are very different from Hemingway, Monroe, and our own Sarah. Sarah chose suicide in an attempt to gain honor. But these people did not try to *gain* anything for themselves!

Witness is the key word. These political suicides felt their dying message would be heard more loudly than any living speech. They wanted to make a public attestation. They were responding to a vision which they believed could be realized for the greater good of the world community.

I'm reminded that in ancient Hindu religions the act of sacrifice was believed to attract the attention of the gods. The sacrificial rite was in short the way to achieve one's desired goals. It seems to me there was that dimension in their suicides—the claiming of some supernatural power by becoming a sacrifice. It certainly seems apparent that these people were doing more than escaping some undesirable situation. They saw one action left to them by which they could attest their vision—suicide.

When a public statement is made through a suicide it becomes a political issue as well as a medical and/or philosophical one. Christine, I mention this because as a person in the health professions, I'm dismayed that suicide is so often viewed only as a disease or illness which can somehow be controlled by medical intervention. (I'm still deeply suspicious of any interpretation that tends to diminish the complexity of suicide as a social/political/ moral/religious act.)

What about the people who kill themselves while in prison? These people can easily be looked at as society's misfits who take the path of suicide as an exit from their prison existence. Or do they in the silence of their deaths make witness to their victimizers? I can't really understand their lives, much less their deaths, because *my* life is so comfortable in comparison, and the sort of injustice I may suffer is something like an inequitable salary scale between men and women. I don't underestimate the importance of correcting such an injustice, but it is not the all-pervading injustice that characterizes many persons' lives. And were I to leave a suicide note, it would be in educated English, typed in my dorm room here in an elitest university on my IBM Selectric typewriter—not scrawled on the wall of a prison cell.

You know, these anti-war and prison suicides raise the question of whether a person in dying by suicide *takes* his/her life or *gives* it. We always talk about suicide as a way of taking life, but some of these protesters give their lives as a witness. They're compelling us to action.

So maybe Sarah does belong among the protesters in the sense that she has moved us to action. The Suicide Prevention Center is now open! And it's surprising how many people have already started to use it. Sometimes I wonder if Sarah knows . . .

By the way, a short note from Geoff! He stopped in Tucson on the way home to talk to young Donald's parents —still mute with grief over their son's suicide. Geoff spent his time finding a counselor to help them work through some of their suffering.

When I think of Geoff, and Donald's parents, and my own reactions to Sarah's dying, and your reaction to Michael's, I'm reminded of something that Arnold Toynbee wrote when he was eighty-five, and most of his loved ones were dead:

> This is, as I see it, the capital fact about the relation between living and dying. There are two parties to the suffering that death inflicts, and in the apportionment of this suffering the survivor takes the brunt.[1]

I send love and the first spring breezes East. Write when you find some time.

Adieu,
Rosa

Dear Rosa,

It was good to get your spring-time letter! It is now the day of Jesus' entry into Jerusalem on the back of an ass with the crowds waving and shouting their welcome. And all the time Jesus knew that within a week, he would be dead. Could he have prevented his own death? Could he have changed the script? Chosen a different path?

Some said he was mad, and treated him with scorn. Later others suggested he had planned the whole scenario quite rationally, that he had been a premeditated martyr, basing all his actions on the Old Testament prophecies. (See *The Passover Plot* by Hugh Schonfield.) It has always been hard for people to understand the giving of one's life for a cause.

I think we are in accord in believing that the deaths of various political and religious martyrs throughout the ages have been in witness to a vision of something beyond the *status quo* to some hope that there is a power or a process of which we are a part and in relation to which our individual lives become of lesser (and paradoxically of greater) importance.

You mention Quang Duc. He was seventy-three when he made his protest against the war (11 June 1963) and the treatment of the Buddhists under the Ngo regime. His rationale must have been much like Charlotte Gilman's—his life had been spent—thus he desired to make his death a truly meaningful act. And it worked. The Buddhists rallied around him in death as they had not in life. They defied the Ngo government by flying flags at half-staff from several pagodas. The United States warned Ngo to act promptly on the Buddhist's grievances. And thousands of Buddhist women and men converged at the Saigon pagoda to pay respects to the dead monk while 10,000 Buddhist youth staged a demonstration which forced the government to release the imprisoned Buddhist priests.

Fifteen days after Quang Duc's suicide, American clergy-people placed an ad in the *New York Times* scoring the Ngo regime's religious curbs; Buddhist leaders demanded the government stop drafting student priests into the army or let them serve as chaplains. In New York City, the Rev. David Harrington of The Community Church, held a memorial service for Quang Duc in which he charged that the Ngo regime was a "vicious dictatorship." The U.S. government began to change its position on the Ngo regime, a regime whose methods it doubted and whose popularity it had finally begun to question.

On 2 August 1960, a second Buddhist priest immolated himself in protest against the Roman Catholic regime's repressive tactics against Buddhists. Ten days later a Buddhist girl in Saigon tried to sever her hand in protest against the government's policies. Two days later a Buddhist student priest burned himself to death near Hué, leaving a letter protesting persecution of his fellow monks. When his brother priests tried to take his body into Hué for burial, they were intercepted by soldiers, beaten, and the priest's body was taken from them. The Reverend Harrington, for the Ministers' Vietnam Committee, sent a letter to President Kennedy urging an end to our support for the Ngo regime; 15,000 American clergypeople supported his request.

Then on August 16, a Buddhist nun burned herself to death at Ninh Hoc and a Buddhist monk immolated himself in Hué pagoda; a third monk ended his life by taking poison. Hué was placed under martial law. Finally President Kennedy appealed to the Pope to intercede with the ruling Diem family to end their repression of the Buddhists. The

Pope sent a message to the Ngo family asking for an end to the persecution. Five days later, heavily armed policemen and soldiers swarmed into four different Saigon pagodas firing pistols, tear-gas bombs, and hand grenades; over 100 monks were arrested.

Well, Rosa, I could go on and on with this sort of documentation—the result of the research I did for a course I took at Harvard on "Religion and the Third World." I am both appalled and amazed at the courage of those monks and nuns who gave their lives in order to preserve the religious and political freedoms they valued so dearly. Previously I'd always thought of *martyr* in predominantly Christian terms.

The first American martyr suicide to make the headlines was that of Norman Morrison, the Quaker pacifist who immolated himself in front of the Pentagon on 2 November 1965. He was considered crazy by many Americans, but in Vietnam he was a hero. Two years later, Nhat Chi Mai, a teacher and social worker in Saigon, burned herself to death in front of the Tu Nghiem Pagoda. Beside her she put two pictures; one of the Virgin Mary and one of Kwan Yin, the Buddhist Goddess of Mercy (a *bodhisattva,* or divine teacher). Her letter to the Vietnamese people said she was doing what Quang Duc and N. Morrison had done. She hung this poem near her:

My Intention

I wish to use my body as a torch
To dissipate the darkness
To waken Love among men
And to bring Peace to Viet Nam.[2]

She lit the flame to her gown and then the fire consumed her body.

I can picture the scene clearly—a noble woman doing a

noble deed. Three years after her death a further wave of protest suicides began in France, this time among the very young.[3]

These suicides began in January 1970, when a sixteen-year-old boy in Lillé doused himself with gasoline and set himself afire in the school playground. He left a note saying: "I offer myself to atone for the wrongs committed in Biafra, against war, violence, and the folly of men."

The following Tuesday, a nineteen-year-old boy burned himself to death in a nearby schoolyard, leaving a note saying: "I did it because I cannot adapt myself to this world. I did it as a sign of protest against violence, to see love again . . ."

On January 24, a seventeen-year-old girl set fire to herself in a Roman Catholic high school in what was described as an exclusive district of Paris. Then she leaped four stories to the street. Hers was the fifth such suicide by fire in France in a week.

According to the *New York Times* report, both the Lillé youths were bright and "apparently normal" students with wide circles of friends, and both were from respected Catholic families. They were not involved in any political group nor were they drug users. The autopsies, which showed no intoxication, stirred great indignation among their classmates. That week hundreds of them marched through the city in a silent procession of mourning. They distributed a leaflet that said: "We cannot remain indifferent before these actions, which challenge us and which also accuse a society that, despite its handsome pseudoliberal mask, has nevertheless forced two adolescents to end their lives so as to make themselves heard and understood."

Both the young Lillé men received church rites. The Right Rev. Adrien Band, Bishop of Lillé, said at the service: "Only God, who gives us life, may take it back. But how can we fail to see that the cruel reality of the world is striking the young. They await our witness, the testimony of our hope and of our engagement."

In our country, the youthful suicide protests I remember most were those of two high school classmates, Craig Badiali and Joan Fox of Blackwood, New Jersey, who killed themselves following a Vietnam Moratorium rally at nearby Glassboro State College and left twenty-four notes urging peace and brotherhood for humankind. One of the notes said, "It seems that people are only touched by death." I also remember the self-immolation of Ronald Brazee, age sixteen of Auburn, New York, who was described by his high school principal as belonging to the top 2 percent in a nationwide test of verbal skills. He set fire to himself in front of the Cathedral of the Immaculate Conception leaving a note which said, "I'm giving my life, not in war, but to help end it. If giving my life will shorten the war by even one day, it will not have been in vain."

As I write this, I feel sick about our society which puts so much onus on suicide and yet participates in large-scale warfare as "one nation under God." What sort of society sees an individual giving up his or her life in protest against an unholy war as a crazy act, but does not see the craziness in the war itself?

It's Palm Sunday, Rosa. How often do those who would point The Way come riding on the backs of asses? And how often, because we do not know them, do we crucify them? (Or force them to crucify themselves?)

I'll mail this on my way to the eleven o'clock service at the Arlington St. church. Greetings to you for Easter Week! Three crocuses bloomed this morning right in front of my eyes. Life goes on and so shall we!

Fondly,
Christine

REFLECTIONS

IN THIS exchange of letters, written in the early spring, Rosa and Christine appear to be rising out of their previous depressions. Their letters show personal hope and a recognition of the possibility of hope rather than despair in the act of suicide.

Rosa refuses to accept the reductionist thinking that suggests that all suicides can be explained physiologically. She points out the absurdity in believing that any action may be "explained" by the biochemical processes which accompany it. "Is a vision *only* a biochemically induced hallucination? Is an act of martyrdom *only* the result of a person's irregularity in the endocrine system?" she asks.

Rosa then writes with much admiration of the self-martyred Vietnamese monk Quang Duc. This leads to a discussion of other contemporary martyr-suicides: among them the Czechoslovakian student Jan Palach and the American Quaker Norman Morrison, who also gave their lives in protest against governmental actions.

Christine replies to Rosa on Palm Sunday. Her tone is optimistic; she expresses her belief that the deaths of the war protestors and the deaths of various martyrs throughout the ages have been in witness to a vision that transcends their present reality, to some hope that there is a power through which individual lives become of lesser (and paradoxically of greater) importance. There is, then, in this exchange of letters a witness to a vision of hope.

For purposes of our discussion here, a *martyr* may be defined as (1) one who voluntarily suffers death as the penalty of refusing to renounce his or her religion or a principle or practice of that religion; and (2) one who sacrifices his or her life, position, or possessions for the sake of principle or for a particular cause. The Anglo-Saxon word comes from the Latin *martyr* and the Greek *martyrs* which probably meant "a witness." The word is also related to the Middle English word *memorie* which comes from the Latin *memoria* and *memor* which meant "mindful." *Memor* was related to the Greek *merimna* which meant "thought, solicitude," to *martys* and to the Sanskrit *samarati* which meant "he remembers." The word "martyr" is, therefore, intimately connected semantically with the concept of remembrance or keeping in mind. We are reminded of Jesus' words, "This do in remembrance of me" (Luke 22:19). Therefore one who defines one's self in an act of martyrdom believes that act to be in the context of a community which will remember and will bear witness to the significance of the act. If this is true, any act of martyrdom must be seen as an act of hopefulness and trust—trust in the reliability of those who remain to make sense of the witnessing-death of the martyr.

Witness is another word in need of discussion. *Wit* is derived from the Sanskrit root *veda*, "I know." The word *witness* may be defined as (1) one who is cognizant by direct experience; one who beholds, or otherwise has personal knowledge of; (2) testimony, attestation to a fact or an event; and (3) one who gives testimony by act of sufferance of fidelity to Christ; a martyr. (This latter usage is considered archaic.)

We have mentioned earlier that martyrdom was often actively sought by the early Christians and when not obtained at others' hands was often procured by one's own action. Martyrdom has also had an honored place in other religious traditions. An old Islamic belief holds that the individual martyred in a Holy War is the only type of person who will spend the intermediate period between death and the Last Judgment in heaven; this person also has the distinction of appearing clothed at the Last Judgment! In Japan, suicide is still traditionally seen as an honorable act of sacrifice, an act of sincerity or *mago koro.* And among the Yuit Eskimos an individual's decision to die in order to save the life of a close kinsman is honored.

In traditional Western religious thought, four conditions are usually thought necessary for martyrdom: (1) The act must be considered rational—that is, thought out, premeditated in accordance with God's will or some Higher Power. (2) The act must be commanded or willed by God or this Higher Power. Augustine, in his *City of God,* allowed that "he, then, who knows it is unlawful to kill himself, may nevertheless do so if he is ordered by Him whose commands we may not neglect" (Book I, chap. 26). (3) The act must be one of "giving" one's life rather than of "taking" it. It is a sacrifice. In early Hinduism the sacrifice was considered even more powerful than the gods and could modify the workings of the entire universe. In Judaism, the idea of sacrifice was central to the history of the people. And Isaiah prophesied that the Messiah would become the sacrifice for all humanity. (4) Finally, in order for the act to be considered martyrdom it must be a statement of commitment to a cause, a cause larger than one's own self-aggrandizement.

Accordingly Bonhoeffer writes, "In the sense of sacrifice, therefore, man possesses the liberty and the right to death, but only so long as his purpose in risking and surrendering his life is not the destruction of his life but the good for the sake of which he offers this sacrifice."[4]

We may consider then the suicides of the war protestors discussed by Rosa and Christine as true acts of sacrifice—if we define *sacrifice* as the surrender of one's own life for the sake of something considered as having a higher or more pressing claim (such as many human lives). Those who gave their lives in protest against the war did so in the belief that the war would end earlier if public conscience were aroused.

Contemplating these suicide-protests seems to be redemptive for both Rosa and Christine. These acts were done not in isolation but in community; they were acts shared by others, deaths planned to have a purging, enlightening, redeeming effect. Rosa and Christine are now, for the first time, in some accord in their judgment of the deed. They agree that Quang Duc, Norman Morrison, and Nhat Chi Mai who *gave* their lives in an attempt to save other lives are people for whom they feel gratitude and reverence.

One question they have not considered at length is the effect these suicide-deaths had on the suicidees' families, a question for which there can be no answer at all or as many answers as there are families. In the case of Norman Morrison, his wife gave out this statement a few hours after his death:

> Norman Morrison has *given* his life today to express his concern over the great loss of life and human suffering caused by the war in Vietnam. He was protesting the Government's deep military involvement in this war. He felt that all citizens must speak their convictions about our country's action.[5]

Accompanying stories explained that Morrison had been a pacifist who seemed to "feel more deeply" than many of his Quaker friends the pain of the Vietnam War, and that, the year before, his friends had talked him out of immolating himself in response to the self-immolations of the Buddhist monks in Saigon.

To the public as a whole, Morrison's death remained a mystery. People began asking if his marriage was unhappy (it wasn't), if he had had a history of emotional instability (he didn't), if he had lost his job (he hadn't). There was, perhaps, a vague sense of guilt surrounding this speculation, a nagging realization that here was a man willing to lay down his life in allegiance to his beliefs and in accordance with his love for others' lives.

The New England poet Emily Dickinson knew about such reactions:

> Much madness is divinest sense
> To a discerning eye;
> Much sense, the starkest madness.
> 'Tis the majority, in this, as all, prevails.
> Assent, and you are sane.
> Demur, you're straightway dangerous,
> And handled with a chain.[6]

Morrison was one who demurred. He declined to accept the majority decision that the war was proper and necessary.

Men like Morrison could be considered dangerous by a government engaged in an act of war (even though the war was not called war) which needed to recruit young men for its ranks, men whose obedience to their military superiors was expected to be unquestioning and absolute. "War may be dangerous to your health" read the signs of the flower children. The signs were often burned or destroyed by other citizens.

What of society's citizens serving time in jails? As Rosa notes many of these prisoners escape their cells through suicide. Are these suicides acts of cowardice? Acts of desperation? Or are they acts of silent protest against the society that has imprisoned them? Acts which declare, "In this final act, I am free again"? To date there have been no definitive studies about prison suicides. The *prima facie* evidence, however, seems to indicate that the suicides of prisoners are most likely to be acts of despair and hopelessness about the future of society and their own lives in that society, whereas the acts of the war protestors and other witnesses seem to be filled with hope that others may come to see the light and that that vision might make life better for all. (All of the information about the motives behind the late Gary Gilmore's prison suicide-attempts has not yet to come to light. One theory is that he wished to die by suicide rather than to set a precedent reestablishing state executions.)

"Seeing the light" has always been symbolically synonomous with "understanding the truth." It is no accident that sacrifices have in nearly all religions been offered up through fire, the symbol of purification and illumination. The attestation to the power of transcendent truth through sacrifice has involved this giving witness through tongues of fire. So Jesus said to the multitudes which followed him, "You are the light of the world. A city set on a hill cannot be hid. Nor do men light a lamp and put it under a bushel, but on a stand, and it gives light to all in the house. Let your light so shine before men, that they may see your good works and give glory to your Father who is in heaven" (Matt. 5:14–16).

For many of the men and women discussed in this exchange, literal self-immolation was the result of their desire to let their light shine in witness to truths which they felt they could see more clearly than their fellow human beings.

CHAPTER 7

THE VAN DUSENS:
A Covenantal Relationship

Easter Sunday Afternoon
Minneapolis, Minnesota

Dear Christine,

Easter greetings from me in Minneapolis! Having stuck it out alone in the dorm during Christmas I decided to fly home for Easter. So here I am in my parent's living room feeling like a little girl again! In retrospect I had a happy childhood—even for a middle child—and Easter was one of my favorite days. But when did it become a symbol of rebirth?

When I was a child Jesus' death (made vivid by pictures and long Good Friday services) was real to me, but the notion of Jesus' coming out of the grave all dressed in white seemed more scary than sacred. I remember when my grandmother died. I was terrified she might try something like that when we went to visit her grave!

It was only as a teenager attending a mountaintop sunrise Easter service that the notion of being reborn after dying began to take shape in my mind as some kind of hope.

Actually, as I remember that year, the idea of getting up while it was still dark to drive to the mountaintop for the Easter service was not very high on my list of priorities. I still remember the bone-chilling hoarfrost dampness while huddled on a thin camp blanket in the blackness, followed by a glimpse of the first crack of light on the horizon. But then I remember being *hypnotized* by that light as it spread upward and around and through us. When at last the sun itself appeared, I nearly shouted with an exuberance that went tingling through my body and into my very fingertips.

I shall never forget that morning. I thought of asking my friends if they hadn't experienced something strange and marvelous when they saw that Easter sun come up, but I was afraid they might think I had really flipped out or something. I remember the tasteless pancake breakfast and everybody talking and laughing as if nothing momentous had happened. So I just kept that vision to myself—that image of the rising Easter sun which symbolized the same resurrection potential which I felt within my own spirit. Imagine, Christine, that was fifteen years ago! And the image still holds for me.

My parents and I have really been talking this week, I mean really communicating! It's hard to see them getting older, but we're so much more compatible now, and you'll be interested in *this:* their church has been conducting a series of workshops this spring, and the one my parents attended was on *suicide.* My Mom said that it was something she didn't know much about and that was why she decided to go. Dad, as an old-fashioned family doctor, has had to counsel several people who have tried to kill themselves, and I know he's never been sure what to say. They both talked about Sarah—who had visited us once—and their horror that she committed suicide so *young.* Then I asked them whether they thought suicide was okay for an *older* person. All of a sudden everyone got very uncomfortable. Mom said that maybe I was dwelling on the subject. And Dad asked if everything was okay with *me!*

Perhaps I knew some of the cause of their discomfort. The event that had stimulated their church workshop on suicide was the death of Henry Pitney and Elizabeth Van Dusen. Do you remember when this couple killed themselves? You must. It made headlines and television, because he was a president of Union Theological Seminary. But maybe you were in England? Anyway, they chose to die from drug overdoses when he was seventy-seven and she eighty years old, rather than to go on living without being able "to do any of the things we want to do." My parents gave me a copy of the suicide letter, which the church had had xeroxed.

> To all friends and relations,
>
> We hope that you will understand what we have done even though some of you will disapprove of it and some be disillusioned by it.
>
> We have both had very full and satisfying lives.
>
> Pitney has worked hard and with great dedication for the church. I have had an adventurous and happy life. We have both had happy lives and our children have crowned this happiness.
>
> But since Pitney had his stroke five years ago, we have not been able to do any of the things we want to do and are able to do, and my arthritis is much worse.
>
> There are too many helpless old people who without modern medicinal care would have died, and we feel God would have allowed them to die when their time had come.
>
> Nowadays it is difficult to die. We feel that this way we are taking will become more usual and acceptable as the years pass.

Of course the thought of our children and our
grandchildren makes us sad, but we still feel that this is the
best way and the right way to go. We are both increasingly
weak and unwell and who would want to die in a Nursing
Home.

We are not afraid to die.

We send you all our love and gratitude for your wonderful
support and friendship.

"O Lamb of God that takest away the sins of the world
Have mercy upon us

O Lamb of God that takest away the sins of the world
Grant us thy peace."

Elizabeth B. Van Dusen
Henry P. Van Dusen

I was deeply moved by this note, Christine. Sitting there
with my parents, I imagined *them* writing to my brother and
sister and me! I asked them if they would ever commit
suicide like the Van Dusens, and they shook their heads.
Dad said, "It's a sin." Mom agreed, but she said she
certainly could see why a couple who had lived together as
long as the Van Dusens had would want to die together. In
fact, my parents sort of agreed neither one would want to
carry on alone without the other, after so many years of
being together.

Then I asked them about their friends in the workshop.
Apparently some might do it if they were in some dire
circumstance—trapped in a burning house, or in excruciating
pain. One man, also a doctor like Dad, said he could see
doing it when he got old. But Mom added that this man's
wife is already dead. And he's in his seventies.

Finally I asked them why they thought the Van Dusens
did it. There was another long, embarrassed silence. Finally I
realized that the whole workshop was identifying closely
with the Van Dusens. Obviously the Van Dusens raised life
and death into a sphere of consciousness that most of them

wanted repressed. The Van Dusens' dying is a kind of witness that no elderly Christian couple can ignore. And I think the most troubling case we've considered, Christine.

In the first place, there is the context in which they took their lives. Quang Duc died in the commitment to a cause. The cause was valued more than the continuation of physical life itself. The Van Dusens died in the context of commitment too, but their commitment was to their *relationship*. They died *together*. Most suicidees choose their path because they feel *alone*. But here we have Henry and Elizabeth Van Dusen killing themselves as part of a cooperative effort, within the context of their marriage covenant, giving every indication that their children and grandchildren are close to them. So now the question is, "Can suicide be seen as acceptable if it is done within the context of human caring and community?" Can a suicide done cooperatively within a covenantal relationship be considered immoral? Parts of the note make me wonder if they really carried out the decision within the covenantal framework and were not just each afraid of being left alone. For instance, one of the most poignant lines for anyone who has worked in such a place is ". . . and who would want to die in a Nursing Home."

Still I'm convinced they had something more in mind than escaping the nursing home (as Marilyn Monroe escaped her unbearable life-script), or that they were simply insistent on dying with dignity (like Ernest Hemingway or Charlotte Gilman). When they wrote "this is the best way and the right way to go," they were suggesting that their act might encourage others down this path. Their tone was one of pilgrims setting out into an unknown but promising direction. They were leading the way for many who might otherwise lack the courage or insight to make this choice. They're somewhat like Sarah taking "a separate path" and, like Quang Duc, dying as a witness to others. They don't

speak of their suicide as a right, like Charlotte Perkins
Gilman did, or like the Stoics, as an exercise of their *right* to
do with their lives as they wished. They belonged to the
Euthanasia Education Council, and in that respect they felt
that it was their human right to die rather than have their
lives prolonged by artificial means.

If the Van Dusens believed that their suicide was the
best way and the right way to die, then I'm really confused.
I am forced to ask, "But isn't *killing* a sin? And isn't suicide
killing? And therefore ISN'T SUICIDE A SIN?????"

Wow! Now I realize THIS IS THE BIG QUESTION.

The Van Dusens said, "We are not afraid to die." Still,
they asked for mercy, "O Lamb of God that takest away the
sins of the world, Have mercy upon us." Do you think that
they took their path believing that it was a sin? But they
also say, "O Lamb of God that takest away the sins of the
world, Grant us thy peace." That makes me wonder,
Christine, if, having seen the Easter sun rise many times on
their lives, they knew that when they took that last step
they would experience the light spreading up and around
and through them just as it filled me on that mountaintop
Easter morning.

Love, and may the promise of new life abide in us
always,

Rosa

Dear Rosa,

I have been sitting on your Easter letter for two weeks now, wrestling with that question in capital letters: ISN'T SUICIDE A SIN?

It's almost embarrassing for us sophisticates of the twentieth century to talk about sin. The word seems archaic. Yet the concept of sin, the belief that some acts are actually sin-full, exists in some deep level of our collective consciousness.

We have spoken of the world being "out of joint," which is another way of speaking of it as being fallen, which is another way of describing us as heirs of the original sin. (How was it the old McGuffey's reader used to put it? "In Adam's fall / We sin-ned all.") I remember being fascinated as a child by my Catholic friends going to confession, and of the distinction between mortal sin and venial sin. If you died having committed one of the former without having confessed, there was little hope for your immortal soul.

The common Roman Catholic definition of a *mortal sin* is one "committed with full knowledge and deliberate intent" in "a serious matter." (Venial sins are not so bad.) But the simpler doctrine I grew up with was that sin was separation from God, a state in which we became strangers to, or es-stranged from, God.

So my answer is that some suicides would be sins and some would not, depending on how they were done and whether or not the individuals saw the acts as uniting or separating themselves from God.

Your Easter Sunday letter was filled, Rosa, with your hope that the Van Dusens took their lives in the light of the peculiarly Christian understanding of the Easter sunrise—of there being a Reality beyond death as eternal as the rising sun.

As I was reading your letter, I was reminded of a dream I had one night two years ago. I'd been driving across Montana (the Big Sky state) where the sun sets quickly and gloriously behind the mesas, and the shadows settle down in deep, blue hues in contrast to the brilliant golds and purples of the sky. The dream I had was this: I was standing on top of one of the mesas and opened my mouth to pray. But no sound came out. Instead a glorious stream of golden light kept rising out of me in a curved bow shape until it reached the setting sun. It was then pulled into the sun and I felt myself being joined to it, taken out of myself and into the sun. I felt no fear, only the joyous knowledge that I was connected to this mysterious source of all power and energy —and that as surely as *I* was now setting, the following day *I* would rise again!

I think the Van Dusens had a similar belief. Your vision of them as "pilgrims setting out into an unknown but promising direction" is beautiful and apt.

It is significant too that their letter was addressed "To *all* friends and relations." This suggests that their act was indeed an act done in community and done for the purpose of witness *to* that community.

I like the phrase, their assertion that "this is the best way and the right way to go." (Could they have been remembering Jesus saying, "I am the way?")

Their final prayer, a traditional part of the communion service, is significant for me. My interpretation of the meaning of communion is that it is in our brokenness that we are brought together in Christ (the breaking of the bread) and it is in our weakness that we are brought to acknowledge the power of God. And it is because of our restlessness with things as they are that we are led (or driven) to find peace in God.

I wonder, for instance, about so many of our great leaders—Martin Luther King, Malcolm X, Gandhi, Dag Hammerskjöld—who continued along their chosen paths even though they were reasonably certain that these paths would lead to their deaths. When Martin Luther King gave his famous "I have been to the mountain top" speech, didn't he surmise that his death-by-assassin was near? Couldn't he have retired into seclusion to save himself?

I am reminded of the story Dr. King told of one of the elderly black women who took part in the year-long boycott of Montgomery, Alabama's buses. When after several weeks of walking she was asked whether or not she was tired, she replied, "My feet is tired, but my soul is at rest." I can see the Van Dusens as feeling tired in their bodies—but finding that their souls were at rest. It was time, in the words of the old Negro spiritual, to "go home to meet their Maker." And that they should go together as they had gone together for so long would seem only natural.

How often one hears of a widow or widower dying soon after the death of his or her spouse! That, too, is considered natural. Another case in point: last summer I read about two sisters who had lived together all their lives; one was eighty-three and one was eighty-two.[1] A community health nurse called on them regularly. One day there was no answer to her ring. She called the police who entered the house and found the sisters dead. The coroner's investigation showed they had both died within the previous forty-eight hours and within twenty-four hours of each other—one of a ruptured ulcer and one of acute bronchial pneumonia. The coroner was unable to determine who had died first. He was quoted as saying, "It's a sad case." But I thought just the opposite: how wonderful that they were so closely tied to one another's psyches that they could die together! And I found myself wanting to love somebody again, so that in our old age we could die together of natural causes. That would truly be *euthanasia,* or "the good death"!

But then what do we mean by natural causes? As Edwin Schneidman has stated, the present classification of deaths is greatly oversimplified. To classify a death as either "homicide, accident, natural, or suicide" is to omit the psychological factors involved, such as the individual's intentions and motivations in his or her own death.[2]

I've just finished reading a fascinating book by Mark and Daniel Jury, called *Gramp.*[3] It's about the death of their grandfather. One day when he was eighty-one, "Gramp" removed his false teeth and announced that he was no longer going to eat or drink. Three weeks later he died, refusing till the end to let his family take him to a hospital. In the final days he told his daughter, "I'm just going to lay here until it happens." There was no sense of his wanting to conquer death, but rather of beckoning to it, saying, in effect, "It is time."

What would it be like if there were no death, Rosa? Jonathan Swift has a wonderful section in his *Gulliver's Travels* about the Struldbergs. They were those special individuals marked from the time of their birth with a sign upon their foreheads which meant that they were to be immortal. Gulliver, when he reaches their land, is ecstatic at the prospect of meeting one of these beings who, he believes, will embody the knowledge and wisdom of the ages. Instead, he finds a band of babbling old men and women who have lost control of both their mental and physical processes. To them, physical immortality is a curse!

"Gramp" obviously understood about such things. He had experienced several instances of memory loss which were to him both frightening and embarrassing, and he held conversations with creatures who inhabited the private world inside his mind. Old-time friends began to withdraw from him. Could it be, as the late Sidney Jourard has suggested, that Gramp was experiencing an "invitation to die" from his friends—so as to save himself the embarrassment of his deteriorating mental faculties?

Back to the question of community! Could it be that the Van Dusens in their conversations with some of their friends had experienced, not the invitation, but the permission to die? And is there not a great difference between permission and invitation? I think so. A community which gives permission to an elderly couple to die together —permission to their sincere and reasoned request—is quite different from a community which gives an invitation to die to an individual or couple who might be causing them trouble or be a burden.

It is in this context I believe, that the Van Dusens chose to make their witness. Among my clippings on them I found this quote most enlightening: "The manner in which the Van Dusens pursued the issue, friends recall, was in keeping with their thorough and frank approach to major concerns. Many friends were accustomed to weighing the merits of suicide without macabre overtones. Consistent with customary parliamentary procedure, a hallmark of Presbyterianism and Dr. Van Dusen's own particular style, various viewpoints were heard and considered."[4]

It seems that the suicide pact was discussed openly at Mrs. Van Dusen's funeral. Yet no public attention was paid when she died immediately after the couple had taken the pills on January 28. Dr. Van Dusen vomited up the pills and died two weeks later, apparently of a heart ailment. (Isn't that an interesting phrase? Perhaps we all die of heart ailments of one sort or another?) Anyway, it was only after *he* died that news of the suicide pact made the news! (They, along with Marilyn Monroe and Norman Morrison, *did* make the front page of the *New York Times*.)

I see the suicides of both the Van Dusens and of "Gramp" (whose family surrounded and supported him till the end) as being thoroughly moral in the sense of being done in loving, responsive relations to others. A clear choice was made, and loving support was given to it.

I do know that when Michael died, I wanted to die. Or a large part of me wanted to die—the part that was Michael's wife. The part that had its identity as being part of a couple. The part that did not want to exist as a "one" in a world made up of "twos." As I told you, the voice of a friend pulled me out of that death pit. And now I find life interesting again. I'm also reminded of a case which has given me great encouragement.

It concerns a former member of the Vermont legislature whose wife Mamie died unexpectedly on a Christmas day when he was seventy-six. Recalling that time, he wrote, "from that moment on life had no more meaning for me. . . . Our love was not simply a compatibility of mind and spirit, but it was intensely physical as well. For fifty-one years, since our wedding night, we slept naked together in the same bed and we enjoyed all the passions and excitements that two powerfully sexed persons induce in each other."[5]

I remember when I first read this account, thinking of the power and the beauty there is in the relationships that truly *do* last forever. Then he described the way in which his life continued to disintegrate (I identified so much with that) until he believed that "death seemed the only way out and . . . perhaps I would find my Mamie there." He tried to asphyxiate himself, but was found by a servant and taken to the hospital. He said that then he began to look again at all his values through Mamie's eyes and thereupon "resolved to live with as much joy as I could accomplish, doing the things I knew she would want me to do. I was still capable of work and there was much that I had left undone. The spirit of my beloved one charged me with the task of fulfilling these, my obligations, and thus I came out of the pit which had seemed so deep and hopeless."

We all know the ancient Indian custom of the widow burning herself to death on her husband's funeral pyre (a custom no longer officially advocated in India). Who can say now in the retrospect of centuries which of these socially approved (indeed, even socially ordained) suicides were wrong and which were right?

Dear Rosa, I look again at your letter, and your question: "Isn't killing a sin?" Maybe we should ask, "Is dying a sin?" And since we all are going to die anyway, how can it matter to a merciful God *when* we choose to do it ("A thousand years are but a wink of God's eye")? Old Ben Franklin wrote in 1749 in his *Poor Richard's Almanac* that "nine men in ten are suicides." Isn't it a matter of the degree of consciousness involved whether we kill ourselves slowly by natural causes or quickly by methods considered unnatural?

Remember T. S. Eliot's line "April is the cruelest month"? It's true! April is a peak month for suicides. It's the month we're also most likely to feel what Chaucer described as "love-longing."

I'm *so* glad you went home for Easter and *enjoyed* the family. Must take off to class now. Write soon.

Much love,
Christine

REFLECTIONS

THESE April letters continue in a generally optimistic tone. Rosa's memories of her Easter sunrise experience and Christine's dream while crossing Montana are both expressions of hope and of connection with the eternally recurring processes of nature.

Yet these letters also ask the very sobering question: "Isn't suicide a sin?" The last Reflections were concerned with the question of whether there is an "unforgivable" sin. We are now faced with the more basic question: "What is sin?" Basically, *sin* has been defined, within the Judeo-Christian tradition, as "separation." Thus, one who is "in a state of sin" is in a "state of separation"—from him or herself, from others, and from God. One who is "saved," on the other hand, is one who is "whole" or at-one-with ("at-oned with") God and the rest of creation. Sin is the sense of separateness, alienation, or es-strange-ment which leads an individual to act contrary to his or her own fullest good and to the good of the whole (or holy).

The question, "Is suicide a sin?" must be approached along the lines of separateness vs. unification. Thus that suicide which is done within the context of human community and in relation to the living presence of God— that suicide is not a sin. By those standards, then, the Van Dusen's suicide may be said not to have been a sin. For their act was a sort of sacrifice within the acknowledged context of a witnessing community. Their suicide note addressed "To all friends and relatives" is a plea for understanding, not for approval. The argument they use is akin to the one used by the eighteenth-century writer David Hume. Hume noted (in *On Suicide*, 1777) that if the shortening of lives interferes with Providence, then medical services are already interfering by the lengthening of lives. Or as a contemporary ethicist notes, "We are, by some strange habit of mind and heart, willing to impose death [i.e., by war and capital punishment] but unwilling to permit it: we will justify humanly contrived death when it violates the human integrity of its victims, but we condemn it when it is an intelligent voluntary decision. If death is not inevitable anyway, not desired by the subject, and not merciful, it is righteous! If it is happening anyway and is freely embraced and merciful, then it is wrong!"[6]

The Van Dusens also observe that medical science has interfered in keeping alive those whom "God would have allowed . . . to die when their time had come." They see themselves as "increasingly weak and unwell" and ask "Who would want to die in a Nursing Home."

There is no hint of guilt-placing or a desire for guilt-provoking: "We have both had happy lives and our children have crowned this happiness." Instead there is a yielding to the natural forces of age: "Since Pitney had his stroke five years ago, we have not been able to do any of the things we want to do and are able to do, and my arthritis is much worse."

There is almost an anticipation, therefore, of the next step in the life process: "We are not afraid to die. We send you all our love and gratitude for your wonderful support and friendship." The letter has the decorum and the cordiality of a politely written thank you, except for the final phrases which echo the words of the communion service, "O Lamb of God that takest away the sins of the world / Have mercy upon us."

Their intent is peaceful. "We feel that this way we are taking will become more usual and acceptable as the years pass." A fascinating article by Robert Kastenbaum of the University of Massachusetts, Boston, would confirm them in this opinion. Kastenbaum writes that whereas "the person who suicides today may be flaunting society, telling us that the kind of life we have made for ourselves is not worth the keeping . . . the person who suicides as part of the designed death in the future would, by his careful and considerate execution of the total act, affirm his respect and participation in our culture's value system. This kind of suicide strengthens rather than assaults the social fabric."[7] This sort of suicide would, according to Kastenbaum, follow "certain cultural guidelines": (1) "an anticipatory period during which usual sociomedical techniques have been given a reasonable chance. Enough advance warning would be given to avoid inflicting the trauma of shock upon the survivors." And, (2) "the 'exit scene' would comfort rather than disturb the survivors."[8] The Van Dusens had attempted to meet these amenities. They had gone through a period of submission to the usual medical treatments for their various maladies; they had talked over their anticipated deed; and they had chosen the most tidy of deaths—an overdose of sleeping pills.

Within their circle of friends and relatives, they had done what they could to prepare for their dying; clearly it was their belief that their act would come as no shock. And there seemed to have been little conjecture later as to whether they could have been talked out of it.

We have discussed the concept of sin as that of separation. Another concept of sin is that of breaking the divine law or violating the commandments. In earlier Reflections, we have noted how Augustine was among the first to claim that the commandment "Thou shalt not kill" prohibited suicide. But modern scholars have shown that the word for *kill* used in this commandment, *ratsach* (Deut. 5:17 and Exod. 20:13) meant *unlawful* killing and was opposed to other Hebrew terms for killing (i.e., for hunger, sacrifice, warfare, and capital punishment) such as *shachat, harag,* and *tabach.* So also in the New Testament, the prohibitions against killing (Matt. 5:21; Luke 8:30; Rom. 13:9) are stated with the verb *phoneuo* the connotation of which is, again, *unlawful* killing, as opposed to such words as *apokteino* and *thuo,* the connotations of which are "to lawfully kill" and "to sacrifice."[9]

Clearly the Van Dusens had *thuo* or sacrifice in mind rather than *ratsach* or murder! And we may even imagine them as part of their covenantal relationship having a last supper not unlike the one Jesus shared with his disciples— sitting down at their table for the last time, blessing their food, and entrusting their bodies and their souls to God.

Karl Barth has written, "Life is a loan from God entrusted to man for His service. There can be no question of paying this price except when a corresponding decree of the Owner and requirement of His service make it unambiguously necessary."[10] From the tone of the Van Dusens' letter it seems that they believed it was right for them to offer up their lives to God at the time and in the manner that they did, as a sacrificial and covenental act.

CHAPTER 8

BISHOP JAMES A. PIKE:
No One Takes My Life From Me

24 May
Berkeley

Dearest Christine!

Good news! I've just been awarded a traveling fellowship for next year! The summer and first term in Edinburgh, Scotland, and the second term in Tübingen, Germany. You can imagine my excitement! I hope to be able to stop in Boston on my way. Will you be there in mid-June?

Today is one of those glorious May days here in Berkeley and I feel as though I could take on the world!

Now, down to earth. Still two papers to get in before the term ends next week; then packing and preparation before I leave June 12. My fellowship begins in the fall, but I want to attend a special summer session in Edinburgh.

What are your plans? Will you teach? I heard from Professor Hunt that you are writing a book! What is it about? You never mentioned a word! Will I see it in manuscript before it goes to the publishers?

I started making a carbon of my letters to you after the first one telling you about Sarah's death, and now I have a complete record of our correspondence. Last night (I couldn't sleep at all) I read over our letters, and was amazed at my discovery. Our letters reflected my experience of grieving for Sarah. I've watched other people struggle to adjust to a loved one's death, and I've experienced my own losses, but I've never had any *record* of the form such grieving takes in my own life and possibly in others' lives. I mean the anger, the depression, the initial denial that Sarah was gone—such as expecting her to answer her phone the next day. Then my dreams about her and preoccupation with my own dying, the guilt I felt about her death, and my involvement in the Suicide Prevention Center. Christine, these are all important and normal grieving activities, and it does help me to be able to look back on them now. Also for the first time since her death I now remember her with real love. I can admit that I miss her. But I'm not torn apart by memories. A healing has taken place, a balm has settled down on my spirit and for that I'm infinitely grateful.

I just heard again from Geoff! He's also recovering. He now feels like moving forward—trying to figure out where he might go from here, whom he might love, how he might best help others who are faced with grief.

Now the sad news—the destructive grief. Geoff told me Sarah's mother attempted suicide last month. He believes it was an attempt that was never meant to succeed. But it's sad to know that she is still in such pain. She wrote a note saying that Sarah's death was probably her fault, and she couldn't live with this.

More news. I saw Paul! I suppose it was inevitable that we should meet again with both of us living in the same city. I had gone to a Chinese restaurant with two friends and there he was, sitting with another woman. My first impulse was to get up and leave, but then I decided, "No! No more running away!" I had a hard time getting through the first course, but then my stomach settled down and I actually enjoyed the rest of the meal. As Paul and the woman were leaving, they came over to our table, and he introduced me to Susan, his friend. Then they were gone. *C'est la vie.* But Christine, I know that if I hadn't told you about my suicidal thoughts following my break-up with Paul I might have been plunged into another deep depression upon seeing him. I was deeply wounded by the death of our relationship, but my letters to you helped the healing. The letters, and time.

Time has been good to me lately! A week ago Sunday was also a beautiful day so I got up early and drove to Davis to visit my friends the Fosters. We attended church in the morning and you can *guess* the topic of the minister's sermon! I was so moved by her sensitivity and forthrightness. She spoke about James Pike, the Episcopalian bishop who perished in the desert. Do you remember? Maybe you even knew him? All *I* know is that he was on what he considered to be a quest for truth and knowledge and that he and his new bride, Diane Kennedy, were searching for the place in the desert where Pike believed Jesus to have fasted and prayed. Their car stalled and they went out into the desert and parted ways in search of help. Several days later Pike's body was found. Officially Pike's death was accidental. But was it? The minister's sermon left me feeling that his death was more than an accident. Christine, it is not so remote, is it, to suggest that suicide might be extended to include many deaths now termed accidental? It is certainly thinking of suicide in broader terms. But the difference between GIVING one's life rather than TAKING it opens up all kinds of new possibilities! I could write another ten pages, but I have an appointment with the dean in ten minutes to discuss the transfer of my credits for next year.

I hope to hear from you before I leave! And to be seeing you soon. If I don't, I'll be sure to send you my Edinburgh address as soon as I have one!

Loving thoughts come your way.

Adieu, friend,
Rosa

Memorial Day
Cambridge

Dear Rosa,

I'm so excited about your news! Congratulations! Scotland and Germany! Can you stop here en route? Or on your way back? I'll be around most of the summer, save for little excursions. You're always more than welcome, I hope you know.

Yes, I'm working on a book on the theme of *attempted suicide* as a sort of symbolic rebirth in such writers as Joan Didion, Sylvia Plath, and Margaret Atwood. Wish me luck . . .

This will probably be my last letter to you before you leave. It's Memorial Day with a big parade and services in the Boston Common to commemorate all the men (and women, I hope) who have given their lives in service to their country. I wonder how many names will be missing from the roster? For instance, will Martin Luther King or Anne Hutchinson be mentioned? Probably not! Yet didn't they give their lives in service to our country as surely as all who have died on the battlefields of our country's wars?

Your mention of the Rev. James Pike is most apropos. No, I never met him, but after reading *Search,* the book his widow wrote about that strange adventure in the desert, I wrote to her. Rosa, she's an amazing and powerful woman, now involved in carrying on the bishop's work and initiating much of her own lifework down in southern California. Perhaps you will be able to visit her someday.

As you may know, at the time of their trip to the Holy Land, the Pikes had been engaged in some controversy with the Episcopal Church. The Bishop of San Francisco had refused to solemnize their marriage (Jim Pike had been divorced); and Pike had been faced earlier with heretic charges for such matters as denying the Virgin Birth. His tenure at the Center for the Study of Democratic Institutions was over; and he was planning to begin a sort of Church Alumni Foundation for people on the fringes of organized religion.

Then this man, whose whole life had been involved in a search for spiritual truths, decided to retrace the origins of his faith by going to the Holy Land and spending some time alone in the wilderness—as holy men have done for so many thousands of years in so many different religious traditions. He said he wanted to write a book about the origins of Christianity.

The month was September. Soon the news broke in the papers. The bishop was missing in the Judean wilderness west of the Dead Sea. The car he and his wife Diane had been driving had broken down on an isolated road outside of Bethlehem. They had both set out in search of help, but he grew tired and she went on, at last finding help at a desert outpost. It was days later before the searchers found Pike's body in a cave.

I'd like to share with you now parts of the letter I received from his wife about this event. She is talking at first about *Search,* written with her brother, Scott.

> I also tried to say clearly—and perhaps I do that most directly in the last chapter, called "No Regrets," that I did feel his death to be in harmony with the over-all pattern of his life, and I feel it to be to that point that you are addressing yourself . . .
>
> I know that nothing in life is "accidental"—and especially

not the major events in a person's life, such as birth and death. . . .

I certainly feel Jim's death was, in that sense, entirely consistent with his life. . . .

For me, the key to understanding lies in seeing that that choosing of the circumstances of one's death is part of the *life* process. It is in the pursuit of life, and in the desire to live our lives in the manner that has meaning to us, and thus is in harmony with our overall life-pattern, that we bring ourselves to the moment of our deaths. Surely this was evident in the Van Dusens' suicide pact. It was because they were so clear about how they wanted to *live* that they could make such a clear decision about how they did and did not want to die. Persons who die *slow* deaths—some deaths seemingly interminable—have also made their choices, choices which have brought them to *their* circumstances as well—be it eating habits, addictions, mental attitudes, emotional patterns, or whatever. Someone who lived as fully and dynamically as Jim did—as vigorously, was bound to die that way, too—totally spending his vital energy in the effort, dying of exhaustion and overexposure. The death could not have been more fitting. . . .

Somehow it has always felt fitting that he chose a place to die where none of us could find him, let alone interfere with his internal process in those final hours and days. . . . I have felt again and again that his death was so perfectly planned that *none* of us were able to interfere with it. . . .

I'd be glad to talk or write further if you want to put any specific questions to me. . . . Meanwhile, I wish you well.

Best of luck to you . . .

With love,
Diane[1]

Her letter reminds me of Jesus' words to his uncomprehending disciples when they questioned his reasons for yielding himself up to the authorities. "No one takes my life from me," he said, "but I lay it down of my own accord." As Diane Pike writes about the Van Dusens, so it was also with Jesus; it was because he was so clear about how he should *live* that he could be so clear about how he should die!

Yes, Martin Luther King and Anne Hutchinson are both great examples of individuals who lived boldly and who also died boldly—their deaths embodying the causes for which they had lived. Should they have been impeded from living out their destinies? What if the same genre of laws which forbids suicide should forbid an individual to continue in his or her line of action or dedication or career once that individual has received a murder threat? What sort of a country would this be then? Wasn't much of the power and beauty of both Dr. King and Anne Hutchinson that they continued doing what they had to do, though they knew that they would die for it? How much of the power and beauty would have been left if they had both stopped what they were doing when the first death threats came?

The phrase "No one takes my life from me," then, implies that no one can take my death from me, either; that is, my death will be a part of my life in ways that, perhaps, only I can understand. And if you try to take away my right to choose my way of dying, you are also trying to take away my right to choose my way of living.

In answer to your question, yes, I'm utterly convinced that the old fourfold classification of causes of death (natural causes, homicide, suicide, accident) doesn't work anymore. I now think *all* death is natural to the extent that we choose *each* action of our lives, including what we eat, what we drink, what we think about, where to go, what kind of work/play we engage in, what kinds of friends to have, etc.

A friend of mine in Gainesville, Florida, wrote to me recently about the death of one of her friends, an amateur cave diver named Bill who was drowned during one of his explorations. Bill had always done something else to make a living for his family, but, according to his wife, his whole life had been his diving. The note that this cave diver left scribbled on a chalkboard slate he always carried with him read:

I GOT
LOST.

TELL CAROL
& THOMAS I
LOVE THEM
VERY MUCH

His mother said, "Bill wasn't afraid of death. . . . What he feared was being strangled by life."[2]

I think, dear Rosa, that's often my fear, too—the fear of *not* being able to choose my own way to die. I often fear the time and manner of my death being predetermined by forces or a Force outside of me.

Does this mean that I deny God's omnipotence? No! But I do believe that if I live my life for/with/and in God, there is no way that I could not die for/with/and in God, even if I choose to end my own life consciously, purposefully, and deliberately.

An old man once said to me, "Our task is not to be successful; it is to be faithful." I must add that our task is not to live to be one hundred, but to live well and bountifully in whatever span of life we have. Bill's mother used the term "being strangled by life." To be strangled is to be unable to breathe. Our Judeo-Christian creation stories tell us that humankind was created when God "breathed into" the first mortal. And thus we speak of all creativity as an act of "in-spir-ation" or of "breathing into." Rather than have the Spirit or in-spir-ation of God cut off from *my own spirit,* while my body lingered on (perhaps in an oxygen tent or an intensive care unit), I would choose to die-in-the-Spirit. Thus, I will continue to live, as best I can, in-the-Spirit. And when I can no longer do that, I'll pray for help from God that I might die-in-the-Spirit.

I am thinking now of the words from II Corinthians 4:7 which Diane Pike chose for the bishop's tombstone in the Judean wilderness: "We have this treasure in earthen vessels to show that the transcendent power belongs to God and not to us." None of us lives forever in this form in the flesh, Rosa. But the treasure of our being-ness is ever part of God, and what is vital is that when we die, *however* we die, we give or yield up that treasure *to* the Spirit instead of trying to keep or take it for ourselves.

Did Sarah take her life, her treasure, her spirit, or give it? What of Charlotte Gilman, Hemingway, Marilyn Monroe, Linda Marie Dunne, Quang Duc, the Van Dusens, Bishop Pike? Perhaps we must end by beginning to admit that we don't know. None of us knows, really, what transpired between any of these individual souls and God in those final, fatal moments. We end, therefore, as we began, with the mystery.

You must come this way en route to Europe. It's time for us to *see* each other again. My best regards to Professor Hunt.

Much love to you,
Christine

REFLECTIONS

IN THIS final exchange Rosa and Christine are seriously
questioning their former concepts of suicide and suggesting a
new definition. Christine goes so far as to suggest that to
the extent we live purposefully and consciously, so shall we
die purposefully and consciously. Thus it may be said that
we all commit suicide in the sense that we all choose,
consciously or unconsciously, the manner of our deaths.
Hence the basic difference between those labeled accidental,
natural, and suicidal is the degree of conscious intention
involved (i.e., those deaths we label "suicidal" are more
often those with the greatest degree of conscious intention).

And Dr. George H. Pollock of the Institute for
Psychoanalysis in Chicago has hypothesized on the basis of
his studies an "anniversary reaction" in individuals, which
means they may consciously or unconsciously "program"
their deaths on the basis of the death time of a loved one.
Dr. Pollock cites Nikolai Gogol, the Russian writer, whose
father became fatally ill at age forty-three; Gogol committed
suicide by starvation at age forty-three. And Vincent Van
Gogh whose brother, born with the same name one year
before Vincent was born, died on the twenty-ninth day of
the month; Vincent committed suicide on the twenty-ninth
of the month at age thirty-seven. Dr. Pollock has also found
that individuals may feel responsible for the death of a
sibling or parent and may commit suicide on the anniversary
of such a death. He cites the case of a fifty-six-year-old

woman who suffered a severe heart attack, but recovered, only to become so obsessed with dying that she consulted a psychiatrist at age sixty-five. She discovered that her father, whom she loved deeply, died when he was fifty-six of a heart attack, and that her brother and her mother were sixty-five when they died.[3]

These studies, though interesting, are by no means conclusive. Yet there is a growing awareness of the interrelatedness between psychological factors and *all* forms of death, and an increasing realization that suicide is *not* an isolated phenomenon. We now know that the "suicide-prone person" is not the only one who "chooses" his or her mode of death, though in the past much research has been directed towards an isolated type of "suicidal person."

More recent thinking has been directed instead towards the question of how death by suicide is *similar* to other types of death. Old categories are being questioned by medical and psychological theorists, and by theologians and philosophers as well. Much archaic theological thought identified death with sin and self-chosen death (suicide) as the unforgivable sin. But now, even these basic assumptions are being questioned. Theology and medicine are both redefining those most basic of questions: "What is life?" and "What is death?"

In this final exchange of letters, Christine considers the last recorded conversation Jesus had with his disciples in the Upper Room, before his arrest and trial. He tells them, as Judas prepares to betray him, "No one takes my life from me; I give it up of my own accord." He implies that he could stop the process that will lead to his death; but he wills not to. Is this choosing-not-to a sort of indirect suicide as Rosa implies?

The letter from Mrs. Pike would seem to confirm Rosa's suggestion. Diane Pike says that Jim Pike's death was "entirely consistent with his life," and that "choosing the circumstances of one's death is part of the life process."

If this is true, is it possible to put ourselves on the road to imminent death and yet remain loyal to the Giver of our lives? The Van Dusens must have thought it was: "O Lamb of God . . . grant us Thy peace." Certainly Socrates as he drank the fatal hemlock believed he was being faithful to that principle of truth for which he had lived. And Jesus hanging on the cross which he himself chose not to avoid called out, "Into Thy hands I commend my spirit." We can imagine that Martin Luther King was doing the same when he assured us, "Mine eyes have seen the glory." And that Bishop Pike did the same in his own way as he died on the desert where Jesus had once walked.

The sociologist, Emile Durkheim, might describe this latter type of (indirect) suicide as *altruistic,* i.e. done because of duty or commitment to a higher power or cause.[4] The more direct suicides which Rosa and Christine have discussed may each find some place in Durkheim's schema. In addition to the *altruistic* suicide (which may describe Charlotte Gilman, the Van Dusens, and all the war protestors and martyrs as well), he also identified the *egoistic,* which results from the individual's lack of integration into society or family life (this could be Sarah), the *anomic* suicide which results from a disruption in the system of sanctions and regulatory devices which control and satisfy the individual's needs (this could also be Sarah or Linda Marie Dunne), and the *fatalistic* suicide which results from overregulation of society and a resulting lack of opportunity for the individual to change his or her role or status within the society (this could be Marilyn Monroe or any of the prison suicides).

The correspondence between Rosa and Christine has had a definite cyclical pattern of its own: death, descent, and resurrection, following almost precisely the seasons of fall, winter, and spring. It began with their reactions of sorrow and guilt at the death of their friend Sarah. After sharing the initial shock, they began to disagree about the meaning of that act and about the basic principles involved in judging a suicidal act. Thus, in their discussion of Charlotte Perkins Gilman, they disagreed as to whether or not one's right to life or obligation to continue living should be based on social usefulness. The Hemingway exchange brought up the question of death with dignity and put them at odds in their consideration of what dignity meant. Did it necessarily mean self-control, independence, the ability to choose one's way-of-being in the world? Christine thought yes, and Rosa argued no.

Their discussion of Marilyn Monroe forced them to ask whether or not suicide could be the only way out for someone who cannot change a script defined by society. In this exchange, Rosa and Christine felt their bonds as women, and revealed more about their own personal experiences concerning the suicide-within-them.

Yet in many ways their intellectual positions were still opposed. So in their discussion of child suicides, Rosa argued that it is the *act itself* which is to be judged, whereas Christine argued that *motive* may well be all.

It is only in their discussion of Quang Duc and the other Vietnamese, American, and European martyrs that they begin to agree that the principles for which one gives one's life may be worth the giving of that life. This exchange begins in the spring and signals a sort of resurrection for Rosa and Christine, both emotionally and intellectually, in the sense that they are beginning to find a new harmony in their views of suicide and beginning to consider the possibility that some acts now labeled as suicide may be a form of hope-in-action and of communal-community-caring.

This new sense of harmony continues through their discussion of the Van Dusens' suicide as action done in the name of a covenantal relationship (based on a covenant to one another, to the community, and to God), and through their discussion of Bishop Pike, as an example of an "indirect suicide" in harmony with a life dedicated to the God-beyond-the-god of all ecclesiastical authority.

What Christine and Rosa have done throughout this exchange has been to look again and then again at their own presuppositions about suicide, the meaning of suicide, the appropriateness of suicide, and as to whether or not suicide may be considered a sin. In so doing, they have challenged many traditional assumptions about the act of suicide and much of their own religious training as to the nature of life, death, and God. They have relentlessly questioned their own first thoughts and the mores and ethics imposed on them by their religious and civil heritage. In so doing, they have helped to continue the ever-crucial process of reform which is vital to the continued existence of the church as an institution.

Christine and Rosa arrive at no final answers. But they have raised significant questions which cannot be ignored by either the churched or unchurched within our society. The theological and philosophical questions they have raised are basic to our changing views of the meaning of all our lives and all our deaths. For it is in continually questioning the old assumptions and truths and in continually breaking through the old ideological boundaries that we find the only truths which we may ever know, the truths of our own beings.

Each of us has a separate path built with the stones of our individual experiences. But all of our paths lead through the same wilderness and to the same final destiny. There is consolation and community in that vision, if we but choose to see it.

EPILOGUE
"Many humans die"

THIRTY-THREE years ago Albert Camus published his *Myth of Sisyphus,* which began with the following statement:

> There is but one truly serious philosophical problem, and that is suicide. . . . All the rest . . . comes afterwards. . . . I have never seen anyone die for the ontological argument. . . . On the other hand, I see many people die because they judge that life is not worth living. I see others paradoxically getting killed for the ideas or illusions that give them a reason for living (what is called a reason for living is also an excellent reason for dying). I therefore conclude that the meaning of life is the most urgent of questions.[1]

It is to answer this "most urgent of questions" that all of the great religions of the world have evolved. And yet, their various and sundry answers have not proved definitive. Today we believers, along with our sisters and brothers who proclaim themselves to be unbelievers, are faced with the realization that there may be no one final, definitive, discoverable answer to the meaning of Life and Death, but only tentative, partial explanations as to the meaning of each individual's life and death. We all have our separate paths.

Thus this book's discussion of suicide has been focused on different individuals and, in particular, on two individuals, Rosa and Christine, who have not discussed "the ontological argument" in the abstract, but who have considered in depth the meaning of suicide in their own lives. They have refused to accept unquestioningly the theological, psychological, and sociological taboos, judgments, and clichés which have, in the past, labeled all suicides as senseless, meaningless, crazy, absurd, or sinful.

They have tried, instead, to suggest that the meaning of each individual's death may best be comprehended in terms of that individual's life. And in the process of their explorations, they have come face to face with the meaning and purpose of their own life–death paths. Much of the purpose of this book will be served if their correspondence has encouraged others to re-evaluate their own life–death paths and to look with more compassion on those of others.

As much of the present literature on death reminds us, we cannot find our lives without facing our deaths. We must, at least symbolically or in our imaginations, lose our lives in order to find them—the old religious truth. We carry our deaths within us, just as we carry our births. We cannot ask the meaning of one without asking the meaning of the other. We cannot ask why people *end* their lives, without also asking why people *live* their lives.

Thus, like so many before us, we must face the Dark to find the Light; we must look into the Void to have a vision of the Whole. It is the vision of death which may enliven us —which may give us courage to open our eyes, to "see again,"to view our lives with new meaning and perspective.

It is such vision that Anne Sexton (who chose to end her

own life) offered when she wrote in one of her finest poems that often unspoken knowledge: "Many humans die."[2] It is such vision that enlightened Anne Sexton to decree in another of her poems: "Listen/We must all stop dying in the little ways."[3]

To live and to die with meaning—is that not what we all are seeking, each in our own way, all on our separate paths?

Notes

PROLOGUE: A VOICE FOR THE VOICELESS

1. Sam Heilig, at the Annual Association of Suicidology meeting in Detroit, 1972, quoted in the *New York Times,* 3 April 1972, 12:1.
2. Sally TeSelle, "An Intermediate Theology," *Christian Century,* 25 June 1975, p. 629.

CHAPTER 1. SARAH: DEATH WITH HONOR

1. *Suicidee* will be used throughout this book to refer to the individual who has chosen suicide as a way of death. The authors conceived of this term to avoid the stigma of the traditional term *the suicide,* and also to dispense with the objectifying effect of the latter term. *Suicidee,* the authors feel, gives the individual the status of an active subject, whereas *the suicide* tends to objectify the person.
2. Edward Arlington Robinson, "Richard Cory," in *The Pocket Book of Modern Verse* (New York: Washington Square Press, 1954), p. 153.
3. All quotations from the Bible are taken from the Revised Standard Version (New York: Thomas Nelson & Sons, 1952).

CHAPTER 2. CHARLOTTE PERKINS GILMAN: AN END TO SOCIAL USEFULNESS

1. *New York Times,* 20 August 1935, p. 44.
2. *Medical Record,* 26 October 1901, 60:660–661.
3. For much of this historical data I am indebted to Norman L. Faberow, "The Cultural History of Suicide," a paper presented to the International Symposium on Suicide and Attempted Suicide in Stockholm, Sweden, 29 and 30 September 1971; published in *Skandia International Symposia* (Stockholm: The Skandia Group), pp. 30–44.
4. Letter to the Editor (name withheld), *New York Times* magazine, 7 July 1974, p. 29.
5. Perhaps the two most notable exceptions are the twentieth-century theologians, Karl Barth and Dietrich Bonhoeffer.

CHAPTER 3. HEMINGWAY: A TIME TO DIE

1. *New York Times,* 2 July 1961, p. 1.
2. Tennessee Williams, quoted in the *New York Times,* 3 July 1961, p. 6.
3. Ernest Hemingway, *Portraits and Self-Portraits* (New York: Scribners), quoted in the *New York Times,* 9 July 1961, p. 45.
4. Sylvia Plath, "Lady Lazarus," *Ariel* (New York: Harper & Row, 1961), p. 14.
5. Sylvia Plath, "Edge," *Ariel* (New York: Harper & Row, 1961), p. 84.
6. Euripedes, "The Bacchae," trans. G. Murray, in *The Complete Greek Drama,* vol. 2 (New York: Random House, 1938), p. 282.
7. Dietrich Bonhoeffer, *Ethics* (New York: Macmillan, paperback ed., 1965), pp. 166–167.
8. Ibid., pp. 167–168.
9. Ibid., p. 166.
10. Ibid.
11. Ibid., 167.
12. Ibid.
13. Ibid., p. 169.
14. Ibid.

CHAPTER 4. MARILYN MONROE: LET HIM WHO IS WITHOUT SIN

1. Fred Guiles, *Norma Jean: The Life of Marilyn Monroe* (New York: McGraw-Hill Bantam Book, 1968), p. 372.

2. A. Alvarez, *The Savage God* (New York: Bantam Books, 1970), pp. 29–31.
3. Bosley Crowther, *New York Times,* 6 August 1962, p. 13.
4. Editorial, *New York Times,* 6 August 1962, p. 24.
5. *New York Times,* 14 August 1962, p. 33.
6. From a paper given by Dr. Joseph Richman and Dr. Milton Rosenbaum at the International Conference on Suicide Prevention, London, September 1969.
7. Ibid.
8. *See* Sidney Jourard, "The Invitation to Die," on *On the Nature of Suicide,* ed. Edwin S. Schneidman (New York: Jassey-Bass, 1969).
9. Edwin Schneidman, "Suicide as a Taboo Topic," in *The Psychology of Suicide* (New York: Science House, 1970), p. 545.
10. Matina S. Horner, "A Psychological Barrier to Achievement in Women—The Motive to Avoid Success," a symposium presentation at the Midwestern Psychological Association meeting, Chicago, May 1968.
11. Fred Guiles, *Norma Jean: The Life of Marilyn Monroe* (New York: McGraw Hill Bantam Book, 1968), p. 376.
12. Fred Guiles, *Norma Jean,* p. 376.

CHAPTER 5. LINDA MARIE DUNNE: TO SUCH BELONGS THE KINGDOM

1. *New York Times,* 7 February 1968, p. 29; 8 February, p. 66.
2. Arthur Kohler and Ezra Stotland, *The End of Hope* (London: Free Press of Glencoe, 1964), p. 252.
3. Sheldon Kopp, *Voices: A Journal of Psychotherapy,* Spring 1972, pp. 38 ff.
4. May Sarton, *Mrs. Stevens Hears the Mermaids Singing* (New York: W. W. Norton, 1965), p. 183.
5. Keith Mono, "A Modish Proposal," *New York Times,* 17 December 1970, p. 47.
6. Greg Brodsky, *From Eden to Aquarius: The Book of Natural Healing* New York: Bantam Books, 1974), pp. 198–199.
7. Dietrich Bonhoeffer, *Ethics* (New York: Macmillan Paperbacks, 1965), pp. 166–167, 172.
8. Karl Barth, *Church Dogmatics,* III, 4 (Edinburgh: T. & T. Clark, 1961), p. 405.
9. Dietrich Bonhoeffer, *Ethics,* p. 166.

CHAPTER 6. QUANG DUC: LET YOUR LIGHT SO SHINE

1. Arnold Toynbee, *Man's Concern With Death* (New York: McGraw Hill, 1961), p. 271.
2. Nhat Chi Mai, "My Intention," in *We Promise One Another: Poems From an Asian War*, ed. Donald Luce (Washington, D.C.: Indochina Mobile Education Project, 1971), p. 111.
3. The following citations are from the *New York Times*, 25 January 1970, p. 6.
4. Dietrich Bonhoeffer, *Ethics* (New York: Macmillan Paperbacks, 1965), p. 166.
5. *New York Times*, 4 November 1965, p. 1
6. Emily Dickinson, "Much madness . . ." in *Selected Poems and Letters of Emily Dickinson*, ed. Robert N. Linscott (New York: Doubleday, 1959), p. 122.

CHAPTER 7. THE VAN DUSENS: A COVENANTAL RELATIONSHIP

1. The San Francisco Chronicle, 9 July 1975, p. 1.
2. Edwin Schneidman, "Suicide as a Taboo Topic," in *The Psychology of Suicide* (New York: Science House, 1970), p. 545.
3. Mark and Daniel Jury, *Gramp* (New York: Grossmans, 1976).
4. *New York Times*, 26 February 1975, pp. 1 ff.
5. Samuel R. Ogden, "When Mamie Left," *New York Times*, 23 January 1973, p. 36.
6. Joseph Fletcher, *Morals and Medicine* (Boston: Beacon Press, 1960), p. 181.
7. Robert Kastenbaum, "Suicide as the Preferred Way of Death," a paper delivered to the American Academy of Suicidology, 1975, p. 22.
8. Ibid.
9. Joseph Fletcher, *Morals and Medicine*, pp. 195–199.
10. Karl Barth, *Church Dogmatics*, III, 4, p. 402.

CHAPTER 8. BISHOP JAMES A. PIKE: NO ONE TAKES MY LIFE FROM ME

1. Diane Kennedy Pike, from a personal letter written to Dr. Linnea Pearson, 27 October 1975.
2. Gainesville *Sun*, 8 September 1975, p. 1.
3. George Pollock, quoted by Justin M. Fishbein in *Family Weekly* (March 28, 1976), pp. 18–20.
4. Emilé Durkheim, *Suicide* (New York: Macmillan, 1951), pp. 282ff.

1. Albert Camus, "An Absurd Reasoning," *The Myth of Sisyphus and Other Essays,* trans. Justin O'Brien (New York: Random House Vintage, 1952), pp. 3–4.
2. Anne Sexton, "Doctors," in *The Awful Rowing Toward God* (Boston: Houghton Mifflin, 1975), p. 82.
3. Anne Sexton, "The Children," in *The Awful Rowing Toward God,* p. 6.